FEB 19 1938

WITHDRAWN

# THE NEW GERMANY

# BY THE SAME AUTHOR

Friedrich Nietzsche und David Friedrich Strauss, 1908.
Der aufsteigende Halbmond (von der jungtürkischen Revolution bis zum deutsch-türkischen Bündnis), 1909.
Friedrich List als Orientprophet, 1910.
Im türkischen Hauptquartier durch Albanien, 1911.
Deutschland im Orient nach dem Balkankrieg, 1912.
Deutschland und die Türkei, 1915.
Werkbund und Mitteleuropa (das organische Prinzip des deutschen Gedankens), 1916.
Deutschland und der Völkerbund, 1919.
Zur Gründung der Deutschen Hochschule für Politik, 1920.
Politik und Wirtschaft—Wissen und Wille, 1922.
Kiderlen-Waechter, der Staatsmann und Mensch, 1924.
Kiderlen-Waechter intime, d'après ses notes et sa correspondance, traduit de l'allemand avec une introduction par H. Simondet, agrégé de l'université, Paris (Payot, Paris), 1924.
Germany and the League (Pamphlet No. 41 of the Foreign Policy Association, New York), 1926.


# OTHER GENEVA SCHOOL LECTURES

POLAND, OLD AND NEW: by R. Dyboski. Oxford University Press, 1926.
THE GOLDEN AGE (a study of the development of American civilization), by Lewis Mumford. Oxford University Press, 1927.

# THE NEW GERMANY

THREE LECTURES
By ERNST JÄCKH

*With an Introduction by*
ALFRED ZIMMERN

OXFORD UNIVERSITY PRESS
LONDON : HUMPHREY MILFORD
1927

DD
249
J3

*To the
Memory of
my only son*
HANS JÄCKH
1900, APRIL 25—SEPT. 16, 1918
*killed in action on the
Chemin des
Dames*

# GENERAL INTRODUCTION

AT the League of Nations Assembly in 1923 it occurred to a reflective onlooker that Geneva, with its wealth of living political experience, was uniquely fitted to become a centre of higher political study.

The idea was followed up by the newly formed International Universities League of Nations Federation, and in 1924 a series of lectures and discussions was organized under its auspices at the time of the Fifth Assembly.

During the following year the plan was developed, and in the summer of 1925 a more systematic educational venture, now known as the *Geneva School of International Studies*, was set on foot during the eight weeks preceding the Assembly as well as during the progress of the Assembly itself; the International Universities League of Nations Federation, still closely associated with the work, generously consented to this extension of its scope and to the consequent change in the type of organization. In the same year the present writer was offered an official position in the new League of Nations Institute of Intellectual Co-operation, and he accepted it on condition that he be left free to continue the work of the School during the summer months.

The aim of the School, it need hardly be said, is not to provide a substitute for the existing forms of national education in international affairs, but to give a special additional training such as no national institution is in a position to supply.

The School of 1925 numbered 579 students from over 30 countries and 115 Universities: that of 1926, 583 students from 29 countries and 116 Universities.

Thanks to the co-operation of many eminent scholars and public men and to the ever-ready collaboration of the League of Nations Secretariat and the International Labour Office, the School is able to command the services of an unequalled body of lecturers, representatives of 16 countries in 1925 and of 25 in 1926, addressing the student body and submitting themselves to the discussion which is a characteristic feature of the life of the School.

Fuller details of the aims and work of the School at Geneva and of its travelling secretaries will be found in the Report on *The Intellectual Foundations of Intellectual Co-operation* issued by the Institute, the programme of the School, and the publications of the International Universities League of Nations Federation (Fédération Universitaire Internationale pour la Société des Nations).

The purpose of the Geneva School Series, to which this volume belongs, is to preserve in permanent form some of the more notable of the lecture-courses and addresses given year by year at the School.

The subjects treated are not confined to politics in the narrow sense of the term; for those associated with the School believe that politics cannot be divorced from other sides of the world's life and that international understanding can be developed most surely by the comparative study of national institutions, national types of culture, and national attitudes of mind.

Geneva is not simply the home of a League of States. It is also the home of a Society of Nations.

It signifies more than the modernization of politics by the introduction of a more effective technique. It signifies also the liberation of nationality by its introduction into a community more responsive to its true demands.

Within these limits, if limits they can be called, the School sets forth no programme, preaches no doctrine, and harbours no conscious prejudice.

For Intellectual Co-operation is based on a broader creed than is contained in the Covenant of the League of Nations itself. It is based on belief in the transforming power of the mind and spirit of man when employed faithfully and unflinchingly in the cause of truth.

ALFRED ZIMMERN,

*Deputy-Director of the League of Nations Institute of Intellectual Co-operation; Honorary President of the International Universities League of Nations Federation.*

INTERNATIONAL INSTITUTE OF
INTELLECTUAL CO-OPERATION,
2 RUE MONTPENSIER,
PALAIS ROYAL, PARIS.

# CONTENTS

GENERAL INTRODUCTION . . . page 7
EDITOR'S PREFACE . . . . ,, 13
THE NEW GERMANY
## LECTURE I
The old Germany and Prussia. — 'Prussian Militarism'. — General Ludendorff and the Emperor. — Parliamentary democracy and monarchistic bureaucracy. — The Chancellor Prinz Max von Baden and a democratic parliamentary monarchy, October 1918. — Final collapse of the monarchy, November 1919. — Struggles of the German revolution against the Russian Soviet. — Struggles of the German republic for the stabilization of Government and currency (Dawes Plan).
pages 17-35

## LECTURE II
The constitution of Weimar, 1919, and the Parliament of Frankfort, 1848-9. — The new constitution 'of the people, by the people, for the people': President, Chancellor, Reichstag, Reichsrat, Reichswirtschaftsrat, the 18 Länder.—Nine parties of the Reichstag and three possibilities of coalition : The concentration of forces lies neither on the right nor on the left, but in the centre. — Stresemann's personality. — Hindenburg's example. — Generals as leaders of the peace movement. — Democracy and responsibility. — The Parliamentary Committee of investigation of the war problems. — The publication of the documents of the Foreign Office. — Political education.— New men control a new machine. — The German School of Politics : Democracy means leadership. — Youth movement. pages 36-69

## LECTURE III
The world revolution of the human mind to-day. — Policy of constructive ideas. — The idea of Right. — German 'Forty-eighters' standing for 'unity and right and liberty', the disarmed peace of Europe, and a League of Nations. — Kant, Goethe, Nietzsche: 'Europeanism' as educational ideal of the Prussian high schools. — Germany's League of Nation's Policy. — The system and spirit of Locarno. — Treaties of Rapallo and Berlin. — European interdependence and Germany as the

interdependent centre. — Antithesis between nationalism and universalism. — Franco-German relationship as fulcrum of the European system. — Disarmament. — Policy of Minorities. — Union of Germany with Austria. — Economic calculation, political experiences, international mind. — Out of the old chaos a new cosmos.   pages 70–102

## APPENDIX

Gerhart Hauptmann's prophecy of Germany's mission for peace, addressed to Europe, 1913.   page 103

## EDITOR'S PREFACE

THE lectures which are here presented in book form were delivered at Geneva on July 12, 1926, and the following days, two months before the entry of Germany into the League of Nations, and it was immediately felt that they should be made available for a wider public. In preparing them for publication some additional material has been inserted, but the form remains substantially that in which they were delivered. Those who heard them will be glad to recall the personality of the speaker as expressed in his characteristic use of our language. Those who had not the privilege to fall under its spell will understand the respect which actuated the decision to present the mould of the speaker's thought as well as the ideas which it enclosed.

Dr. Ernst Jäckh is well qualified to bridge the gulf between the Old and the New Germany.

Born in Wurtemberg, like his friend Kiderlen-Wächter, he studied in German universities and at Geneva, and began his political career by editing the oldest democratic paper in South Germany. He associated himself closely with Friedrich Naumann, the Christian Socialist leader, and was instrumental in securing his election to the Reichstag. Since 1902 he has been a leading figure among German Liberals, being on the executive of the Democratic party and a member of the National Economic Council (Reichswirtschaftsamt) set up by the Weimar Constitution.

In the sphere of foreign affairs he is known as the friend and confidant of Kiderlen-Wächter, whose too brief tenure at the Wilhelmstrasse ended in 1912. Dr. Jäckh's two volumes containing Kiderlen's intimate papers are familiar to every student of the origins of the war.

During the war he was employed on numerous missions in Turkey (which he knew well from previous residence), the Balkans, and elsewhere. Reminiscences of these activities, which brought him up against the realities of the old German constitution, are to be found scattered through these pages.

But for Dr. Jäckh, as for so many Germans, the war proved not an end but a beginning. His real life work was only discovered after the Armistice. It is the German Institute of Politics (Deutsche Hochschule für Politik) founded by him in memory of the young life to whom the volume is dedicated.

The Hochschule, which is closely linked by ties of common aims and common methods with the Geneva School of International Studies, has realized with characteristic German thoroughness the idea of political study as a collaboration between the world of thought and the world of action. Academic in its standards and in the quality of its teaching body, it maintains its contact with the larger laboratory by calling regularly on the services of some of the leading actors on the stage of German affairs. An institute of University rank which can count on regular courses by the Chief Justice, the Foreign Secretary, and the Governor of the National Bank is more than a sequestered grove of academic reflection.

Dr. Jäckh believes that the way to avert another war is to increase the amount of intelligence systematically devoted to public affairs; and he believes that the way to mobilize this intelligence is to provide a living national centre for political study. From that to the idea which inspired the founders of the Geneva School is but a single step, and the *amicabilis concordia*, to use the old academic term, which exists between Geneva, Paris, and Berlin to-day is a characteristic manifestation of the new spirit that is now growing up and taking practical shape not in the New Germany alone but throughout the continent of Europe.

A. Z.

Only look upon things from a different point of view from that which you have hitherto been accustomed to, for that means beginning life anew.

MARCUS AURELIUS.

It may be that God is planning another era of desolation for Germany to be followed by a new age of glory; this, of course, on a republican basis.

BISMARCK.

# I

IN endeavouring to describe the new Germany in a short course of lectures, I purposely make a distinction between facts and problems. Facts are the basis for the formation of judgements, and it is only a judgement founded upon present-day facts and figures that is capable of envisaging the problems scattered along the high road leading to the future. I cannot, of course, within the limits allowed me, enlarge upon every fact and every problem. I can merely sketch the broad outlines, and hope that the subsequent discussion will give you and me an opportunity of elaborating the rough general sketch with sufficient details, so that ultimately a clear and well-defined picture of a new Germany may be obtained, of her difficulties and her achievements, her intentions and her aspirations.[1]

The first fact is: A new Germany *does* actually exist, a new body and a new constitution, a new spirit and a new conviction.

As you know, there was a time when 'Germany' was simply a geographical term—before and up to 1870; even as recently as 1866 there was war in Germany, between North and South, between Prussia on the one hand and Austria, Bavaria, and Wurtemberg on the other.

Then Germany became a political term—from 1871 to 1918; but yet it was not really Germany, but only an enlarged Prussia, a Greater Prussia—a Prussian hegemony, established by the German constitution. A characteristic illustration of this is the recent discussion on the subject of compensation for the former ruling princes. The question

[1] I shall not deal with the economic problems, which are reserved for the lectures of my colleague, Dr. Hirsch.

of compensation for the German Emperor does not arise; it is purely a question of the King of Prussia. It is only in his capacity as King of Prussia that he possessed personal property and real estate, not as Emperor. The Emperor did not receive a salary: Emperor implied title and power but no appanage.

Even Bismarck once went so far as to declare that Prussia must be Germanized. In fact, it was just the reverse that happened: it was not Prussia that was embodied in or assimilated by Germany, but Prussia that mastered Germany.

Another Chancellor, Prince Hohenlohe, said: 'It was my duty to work in Berlin to keep Prussia in the Reich, which all these Prussian gentlemen would throw over any day. Why? Because the ruling classes and their camp-followers of more humble origin are incapable of accepting the principles of true democracy with all its social consequences.'

And finally, the Chancellor Bethmann-Hollweg, after the world war and the collapse of the empire, declared that 'The crudeness and immaturity of our political development had become a curse to us'.

In other words, the Germany that emerged from 1871 was not complete as Germany, but had become and remained simply an enlarged Prussia, a Greater Prussia. It was and remained the outward and visible sign of the political predominance of anti-democratic Prussia over a Germany occupied in democratizing herself, the political predominance of Prussia with its anti-social plutocratic franchise and the leadership of Conservative 'Junkers' over a Germany with its universal equal franchise and Socialist workers' organization.

To-day Germany is solidly established with a German constitution and relieved of Prussian predominance.

What is the measure of the change?

Let me give you a personal reminiscence.

During the war I had several political missions which took me to General Head-quarters. I met the Emperor and the Chancellors, Admiral von Tirpitz and General Ludendorff, and other leaders, and repeatedly conversed with them on political questions. What did I find? Every one of these political and military chiefs in his own house, separated from each other, working against one another, every house surrounded by an intellectual barbed-wire fence and by intellectual poison gas. This system was the result not of personal intrigues, but of the independence of each branch of the Government, as guaranteed by the former constitution. The Chancellor was not Prime Minister, but only an individual of equal rank with thirteen other chiefs and colleagues, mostly Prussian ministers and Prussian generals.

In effect this ostensible equality involved the supremacy of 'Prussian militarism' over German policy—both as regards historical development and the mentality of the subject classes.

What, in fact, was 'Prussian militarism'?

Prussian militarism was established 150 years ago by the father of Frederick the Great as the necessary organization of a sparsely populated country without natural frontiers. It was the making of Prussia, and through Prussia made Germany possible. In the light of history it appears that there was only one way, the Prussian way, that could have led to a united Germany; that is why, a hundred years ago, even the non-Prussian leaders of Germany were serving Prussia: men such as Stein and Scharnhorst and Gneisenau. They believed in the German mission of Prussia: they longed for a future Germany to be achieved through Prussia. Likewise Paul Pfizer, a Wurtemberg publicist, in his *Correspondence of Two Germans* (1831), argued that Prussia alone, with her powerful army and her efficient bureaucracy, could lead Germany to the creation of a National State. But in 1848 the Prussian King triumphed over the revolutionaries of German liberalism, and in 1871 Bismarck, whilst giving the German Federal State the universal and equal parliamentary franchise, associated it with the political hegemony of Prussia. Thus Prussian militarism gained the upper hand more and more, without, however, retaining the spirit of its founders or former leaders. Historically speaking, militarism was the natural system of a Germany which had the largest population and the smallest territory among the European Powers, as well as the worst strategic position at a time when all States were convinced of the necessity and possibility of national security based on military organization, and when universal military service had been created by the French Revolution.

'Prussian militarism' was a fact—not in the sense of military armaments in Germany being more extensive or more powerful than those of other Powers. On the contrary, a comparison of military armaments in 1914 shows that the war strength of Germany was less than that of the other neighbouring great Powers.

Lloyd George (in January 1914) said that 'The German army is vitally important not only for the existence of the German Empire, but also for the very life and independence of the German people themselves, since Germany is, as a matter of fact, surrounded by other nations of which each possesses an army practically as strong as that of Germany herself'.

'Prussian militarism' was a fact—but not in the sense of the German General Staff having provoked the war.

Those who knew General von Moltke personally know that at heart he was really something of an intellectual 'pacifist', that he looked upon his duty of mobilizing as a terrible misfortune, a tragic stroke of fate. His *Reminiscences*, too, bear witness to this fact.

Those who have read the memoirs of the chief of the Austrian General Staff, Conrad von Hoetzendorff, know that this general, who for the sake of the preservation of the Austro-Hungarian monarchy considered a preventive war necessary even some years before the world war, reported on his Berlin impressions of 1913 in a very disappointed vein, summarizing them in a sentence to the effect that the Berlin generals did not want to have anything to do with a war of prevention. He actually says 'that although Germany was reckoning with the inevitability of a war, she had not made up her mind to play her cards to that end, being content to let events take their own course'.

Mr. Lloyd George was quite right when he stated (in December 1920) 'that not one of the leading men really wanted war. They slipped into it, as it were, or, better still, they staggered and stumbled into it, perhaps through their own folly. I myself, at any rate, have no doubt that a conference would have prevented war.'

Finally, President Wilson admitted too (on the 16th of October 1916) 'that no one single outstanding fact caused the war, that really the graver blame rested upon the whole European system, a concatenation of alliances and treaties, a complicated network of intrigue and espionage which unerringly caught the entire family of nations in its meshes, so that an explanation for the war is not such an easy matter, its roots extending deep down into the dark recesses of history'. President Coolidge, too, has expressed himself much to the same effect.

Nevertheless, 'Prussian militarism' was a fact—in a far deeper and much graver sense, that is to say, in its supremacy over the German Government.

Even Bismarck had to suffer from it and fight against it. You will remember the occasion when, in 1866, he wished to call a halt to the victorious Prussian army after the battle of Königgrätz, and met with opposition on the part of the Prussian generals, who wanted to march into Vienna. The discussion was so difficult and acrimonious that Bismarck actually thought of committing suicide; eventually he succeeded in making his policy of reconciliation with Austria prevail against General von Moltke with the King of Prussia, although not without the King describing the Peace of Nikolsburg forced upon him in this way as a 'dishonourable peace'. You will also remember how, in 1870, Bismarck, whilst at General Head-quarters, complained again and again of the preponderance of the generals, and that ultimately when concluding peace he succumbed to them and gave way on a very important question—that of the annexation of Metz, to which he was opposed at first on account of its French element.[1] In his discussions with the military authorities, Bismarck enjoyed many advantages which his successors lacked: among others a sovereign who had confidence in him, and in the end allowed himself to be guided by him, and a colleague, General von Moltke, who was his personal friend, and who was capable of thinking in political as well as in military terms.

But what was the situation when 'militarism' became a synonym for Ludendorff, a general without any political instinct whatever? That was my own first personal impression, when I met him for the first time at General Head-quarters, and had to discuss political problems with him. And that was also my last impression when, in March

[1] Bismarck pointed out: 'We do not want Alsace-Lorraine. France may keep these provinces under conditions which render them useless to her in case she makes war against us.' 'I do not want the annexation of Alsace-Lorraine. . . . But the generals think Metz necessary for us because it represents for us the equivalent of 120,000 soldiers.'

## LECTURE I

1918, he wrote me a letter in reply to a petition which several political friends of mine (Friedrich Naumann, Max Weber, Robert Bosch) had addressed to him, in which we submitted our political reasons against his last military offensive before he undertook it.[1] And those who read the Minutes of the meeting of the 8th of January 1917, in which the military authorities decided upon the ruthless submarine war, in the absence of the Chancellor and in the face of the Chancellor's misgivings, will be absolutely dumbfounded at the lack of political reasoning revealed therein.[2] As regards the general public, the fact of the political incapacity of Ludendorff was not manifested until after the world war, when Ludendorff began to prepare his domestic 'putsches' (*coups d'état*)—without the faintest knowledge of the political forces in the German people, and consequently without the slightest prospect of success. At that time the disappointing impression of Ludendorff's political incapacity was expressed in the significant tone of the popular judgement: 'Now we know why we lost the war.' In other words, if a man capable of such political errors of judgement was the real controlling force, then ultimate defeat was a foregone conclusion.

I have already alluded to one difference between the respective powers of the political and military leaders at the beginning and end of the old régime—the personality of the King and Emperor William I and that of his grandson William II: the former amenable to the advice of a Bismarck, and restraining the will of the military faction; the latter in discussions with Bethmann-Hollweg and the other German Chancellors on the one hand, and the forces of Prussian

---

[1] Ludendorff's letter is dated 22nd of February 1918, and has been published in my review, *Deutsche Politik*, No. 18, 1920.

[2] Cf. the protocol of the decisive meeting, 8th January 1917, in *Die Tragödie Deutschlands*, Verlag Duncker & Humbodt, Leipzig.

militarism on the other, giving way more and more to the latter, succumbing, yes, even forced into impotence by them. I remember a friend of mine who was the chief of the Civil Cabinet of the Emperor, Herr von Valentini, a Conservative by origin and a Liberal by experience, indeed too Liberal for General Ludendorff. Ludendorff compelled the Emperor to dismiss Valentini. When he dismissed him, the Emperor addressed another chief of the Imperial Cabinet, Herr von Müller, also a man with modern ideas, saying, 'My dear Müller, I do not know how long I shall be permitted to keep you with me!' During the course of the world war the Emperor, after having been the central figure of the political and military scene, became more and more insignificant, and actually a tool in the hands of those who sought the predominance of Prussian militarism. As a matter of fact, William II was more weak than wicked.

This state of affairs made possible what actually happened, namely, that the first decision in favour of the submarine war was wrung by an admiral from the Emperor, without any cognizance whatsoever on the part of the Chancellor. And is it not absolutely incredible that during the war no Chancellor knew how many submarines Germany possessed? Chancellor Bethmann-Hollweg only learned the facts several years after the war, in the same hour as I myself (a member of the investigation committee of the Reichstag), on the occasion of a hearing before this committee. Another fact: During the war Chancellor and Emperor desired to alter the electoral franchise of Prussia, because they considered it plutocratic as well as unjust; they desired to democratize it, but General Ludendorff forbade and prevented such action. At another time during the war the Chancellor spoke in the Reichstag in the interest and furtherance of peace, but representatives of Ludendorff, who were in charge of the censorship, forbade and prevented the publication of that speech in some districts (such as Cassel). And in the end it is not surprising that General Ludendorff could force the dismissal of Chancellor Bethmann-Hollweg, because he was not sufficiently militaristic for him. Ludendorff also caused the removal of the Minister of Foreign Affairs, Kühlmann, because he pleaded for a peace of Right and not of Might; and finally, General Ludendorff was instrumental in bringing about also the removal of the Chief of the Emperor's Cabinet, von Valentini, because he deemed his tendencies too liberal. And so on.

In this way developments had turned everything topsy-turvy: in peace-time the chief principle laid down for the conduct of an officer was, that he should not meddle with politics, and in war the self-same officer suddenly framed policies of his own and arrived at decisions—without the slightest conception of the fundamental difference between military and political reasoning. Military mentality is a reasoning of might, of 'military necessities'; political mentality is a reasoning of ideas, of political possibilities. Military reasoning led the military authorities to the violation of the neutrality of Belgium and nearly led Ludendorff on to the violation of the neutrality of Holland, which the Emperor prevented in February 1918.

What is the position in States governed by a parliamentary democracy? The Prime Minister is the chief and responsible head. He is also chief of the military forces. He in actual fact applies the classical dictum of General von Clausewitz that war is merely a continuation of politics with other means. He decides the political goal to be aimed at, and it is he also who subordinates the direction of the military operations to that political goal. The political chief appoints generals and dismisses them. It was Napoleon who said: 'Nothing is more important in a war than unified leadership under one single chief.'

And what was the position in war-time Germany with its monarchistic bureaucracy? Here the Chancellors of the Reich and even the advisers of the Emperor were appointed and dismissed by a general; here the military authority also determined what the political goal should be and decided the issues. Here the Chancellor of the Reich was not the chief; he was merely a colleague in an association, an association of officials, composed of thirteen authorities or officers besides himself of whom six were military, one imperial, and six Prussian. The six military authorities were: the Prussian General Staff, the Prussian War Office, the Military Cabinet of the Emperor, and three Naval Departments. Imperial affairs were represented by the Civil Cabinet of the Emperor; and then there were six Prussian ministries. Not a single minister of the German Reich could be a member of this association, simply because Germany as such had no ministers, being merely represented by the Chancellor, who at the same time was also the Prussian Premier. Not even the German Secretary of State for Foreign Affairs at the German Foreign Office could be a member. The military and the Prussian civil authorities had direct and immediate access to the Emperor, likewise also Commanding Generals, but no German Secretary of State, not even the Secretary of State in charge of the German Foreign Office. Similarly the reports of the military and naval attachés of German embassies abroad had direct access to the Emperor, but not the reports of the ambassadors themselves. There was another very important point: the greatest power in the State, the army, was not included in the constitutional organization of the State at all. The appointment of military chiefs and officers was not even effected by a ministry, not even by the Prussian War Ministry, but through the Military Cabinet of the King of Prussia, a central office under the immediate orders of the monarch, which since 1883 had been raised to the status of an office with direct access to, and taking its instructions direct from, the monarch. That meant, that as regards the composition of the corps of officers, constitutional forms, even Prussian constitutional forms, were entirely eliminated.

Such was the supremacy of Prussian militarism over the German Government.[1]

Now you will understand the epithet that the Liberal Crown Prince Frederick applied to the German constitution: 'An artificial chaos.' And now you will also understand what a Secretary of State—a Conservative—meant when, on the strength of his own experience, he once said to me at General Head-quarters: 'A state coach to which thirteen horses have been harnessed, none of them trained in harness together and all of them kicking over the traces, could not possibly run smoothly—not even with a genius like Bismarck as coachman.' And yet Bismarck had not to reckon with the three navy departments; they did not exist in his time.

And now you will understand what Bethmann-Hollweg meant by saying: 'The crudeness and immaturity of our political constitution has become a curse to us.' And you will also understand the historical significance of the real political revolution in Germany—not that of November 1918, but of October 1918—the revolution of the German

[1] Ernst Troeltsch thus characterized this system (November 16th, 1918): 'Militarism was the construction of the State and Society on the Prussian military system and the spirit which corresponds to it. German militarism did not consist in a powerful army or a penchant for Imperialism, which were common to other States. It was rather a political institution, the deciding element in the Constitution, since it formed the essence of the ruling society. The German Constitution was a dualism, for behind the civil government, consisting of the Reichstag, the Bundesrath and the Ministers, stood the military power of the King of Prussia and the General Staff. The system was rendered tolerable by general prosperity and a model bureaucracy; but it had no roots in the people, and it was broken in pieces by defeat.'

Chancellor, Prince Max von Baden, expressing the revolt of the civil power against Prussian militarism.

The military defeat of militarism was the cause of its political dethronement. The Chancellor, Prince Max von Baden, a southerner, heir to the Grand Duchy of Baden, proclaimed a new German constitution, establishing a democratic parliamentary monarchy in the place of a bureaucratic militaristic monarchy, with a constitution modelled on the English system, balancing monarchy and democracy against the supremacy of Prussian militarism. This new constitution was approved by the Emperor and passed by the Reichstag; it involved a revolution in the government of Germany. It transformed the Chancellor from a weak colleague of Prussian generals and ministers into a real Prime Minister with authority over all officers, whether civil or military. It deprived the King and Emperor of his Military Cabinet and of the supreme command, as also of the right to appoint generals and officers, placing them under the control of the Chancellor and of the German Parliament. It gave Germany parliamentary government, providing the Reich with an extension of the authority and privileges of the Reichstag, and Prussia with the universal and equal franchise. It raised Alsace-Lorraine (upon the division of which the King of Prussia and the King of Bavaria had agreed during the war) to the status of an autonomous federal State, and proclaimed as its foreign policy a programme of peace and the establishment of a League of Nations. So Chancellor Prince Max was quite justified in saying, in a Note addressed to President Wilson, that 'The new German Government is a government of the people, in whose hands rests both actually and constitutionally the authority to make decisions. The military powers are also subject to this political authority.'

That was the real political revolution ushering in the new Germany. The parliamentary monarchy of Germany, the consummation of which was prevented in 1848 by force of Prussian arms, which broke up the first German Parliament of Frankfort in St. Paul's Church;[1] the parliamentary monarchy of Germany which later on was prevented by the successes of Bismarck's foreign policy, successes which won over Liberal and democratic citizens to the monarchical idea of the Hohenzollerns, was now proclaimed as the outcome of the defeat of this military monarchy. The war, from the very start, was a 'forcible teacher', the educator for democracy. Both Emperor and Chancellor, at the very beginning of the war, had recognized the necessity for a new order of things in government—a development of democratic and social conditions in consequence of the achievements of a people in arms, and had solemnly proclaimed such a new order. But again and again in their attempts at reform they both suffered shipwreck on the rock of Prussian militarism. Now the defeat of the autocratic States and the success of the democratic States were manifest to the world. Walter Rathenau said: 'The war appears to me as the world revolution against the relics of autocracy and feudalism in Central and Eastern Europe.'

But this October revolution from above came too late.

This 'too late' reminds me of a true story. During the war a political mission took me from Berlin to Warsaw. In a dining-car I met the German Vice-Chancellor and an Austrian Prince. Both partook of a sumptuous meal and a bottle of champagne, and were so deeply engaged in a political discussion that they did not notice that the train had stopped. By accident the Vice-Chancellor looked out of the window and saw a group of soldiers staring at their laden table with

[1] Compare pp. 36 ff.

hunger and envy in their eyes. The Vice-Chancellor put the bottle under the table, in order to remove it from the view of the soldiers. This caused the Austrian Prince to remark: 'Typically German, correct but too late.' This 'correct but too late' was true of many decisions of the old bureaucracy. The November revolution from below broke out, partly as one phase of development from the October revolution from above, as we now know from the investigations of the Parliamentary Investigation Committee.

What happened? In October 1918 the Admiralty prepared an attack of the German fleet against the British fleet —again without the cognizance of the political Chancellor and in spite of the new constitution, indeed, intentionally in opposition to this new order. The fact that the Chancellor of the Reich was not informed of the intention of the Admiralty, and that his consent was not applied for, was a demonstration, a political rebellion of the Admiralty against the new constitution, which had made the Chancellor of the Reich the chief of the Admiralty also. Several sailors, socialistically and democratically inclined, recognized the state of affairs. They heard and knew of the attitude of the officers in opposition to the new democratic constitution, in opposition to the People's Government, embodied in Chancellor and Parliament and agreed to by the Emperor. So the sailors demonstrated and rebelled in favour of the new democratic constitution against the Admiralty, to whom they refused obedience. They were ready to defend Germany, but not to attack Great Britain at a time when the political Chancellor asked for peace and armistice. Together with other causes and reasons, that was the decisive signal[1] for, and the beginning of, the revolution

[1] Cf. the report of the trial of the sailors before the court-martial in *Der Marine-Justizmord 1917 und die Admirals-Rebellion 1918*, Verlag F. H. W. Dietz Nachf., Berlin.

of November 1918, the signal for the rapid and complete collapse of the military monarchy, of a system which had so far outlived its strength that it dissolved in a night, died, without a death struggle, like an oil lamp that goes out for lack of oil, without a breath of air to blow it out. This revolution was rather a negative than a positive movement the outcome rather of disgust than of enthusiasm.

The struggles of the revolution during the winter of 1918-19 were not directed against the old form of military and bureaucratic monarchy (which had vanished overnight), but against the new form of the Russian Soviet; and the protagonist and defender of the new Germany was the spirit of Prince Max's constitution based on the democratic will of the labouring classes and of a portion of the liberal bourgeoisie—a will to a parliamentary democracy; but now no longer in the form of a parliamentary monarchy (since the monarch himself had disappeared), but in the form of a parliamentary republic.

The life-force of the new Germany was the parliamentary constitution of Chancellor Prince Max, but the young Germany, like every child, had first to pass through an embryonic period—of exactly nine months—from November 1918 to August 1919, up to the date of the new constitution of the Reich, established by the German National Assembly at Weimar on the 11th of August 1919.

That is the official birthday of the new Germany, the entry in the birth-register. The nine months of the embryonic period are crammed full with the struggles and convulsions, the difficulties and pains, incidental to an embryonic period, the struggles of a democratic Germany —not against the monarchical nationalistic Germany (which ventured to show its head again a little later when this attempt was no longer dangerous), but against a Bolshevistic Soviet, a republic of workmen's councils on the Russian pattern, which was endeavouring to establish itself. These struggles were especially arduous and dangerous for the provisional Government, because demobilization had rendered it defenceless and the terms of the armistice had disarmed it, whereas the Bolshevistic organization was armed and powerful. When the first Bolshevistic revolution broke out, the only resource of the Government, with no troops behind it, was to crowd the streets around the Government buildings in Berlin with human beings, bodies of men and women, girls and boys, for a day and night, for the purpose of protecting the life of the Government against the armoured cars of the Communists. This saved the Government, for the German Communists were not at heart like the Russian Bolshevists, and would not fire on defenceless people.

It will always be to the credit of Ebert, at that time labour party leader and later on People's Commissary, that by personal courage and political sagacity he defended and saved Germany and Europe against the danger of Bolshevism threatening from Russia. This credit is shared with Ebert by Hindenburg, at that time Field-Marshal and to-day President, who on the first day of the revolution placed himself at Ebert's disposal for the preservation of order and unity, in the same spirit of loyalty which later on made him President—the spirit of service to the people.

And now let me add hurriedly, in broad outlines, something about the development of this new Germany up to the present time.

From November 1918 to August 1919: the weakness of the embryo. Then from August 1919: the Weimar constitution, up to August 1924, the date of the Dawes plan, the five years' infancy of the young Germany, years of childhood and childish diseases. The new Germany was born—'born in tears and blood, baptized in blood and tears'. It was a weak and sickly child! Afflicted with all the known and unknown diseases of children, feverish and hungry; its life menaced by every kind of danger.

In its domestic policies Germany was endangered by counter-revolutions. In its foreign policies Germany was bound and humiliated by treaties, which were not agreements but ultimatums and dictates, from the Treaty of Versailles up to the Ultimatum of London.

This whole childhood is a struggle for stability: (1) for the stability of the régime: of the republic against Bolshevistic and communistic 'putsches' and against monarchistic and nationalistic 'putsches' also. Liebknecht and Ludendorff are the prototypes of this period.

(2) A struggle for the stability of government: of the political authority against the egoism of the economic leadership, against the misleading and disruptive catchword or party cry about the 'economist expert', who in reality is nothing but an interested party; against the disestablishment of the State by the economists, who unconsciously confounded *res publica* with *res privata*, the commonwealth with private interests. A significant prototype was Hugo Stinnes.[1]

(3) A struggle for the stability of the currency, the foundation-stone of all economics and politics, of the very

[1] The National Federation of German Industry was at that time under the influence of Hugo Stinnes, but what an evolution in three years! Now (1926) the National Federation of German Industry gives its approval to an application based upon the principles of the German Republic and the Weimar constitution, advocating economic and political co-operation between employers and employed (Trade Unions and Social Democracy). A leader of the Catholic Trade Unions says in this connexion: 'I consider this step taken by German industry of equal importance to the social message delivered by the young emperor in 1890, only with this essential difference: that now it is not a monarch that is speaking, but the organization of German industry as a whole.' Even a German Nationalist critic is forced to admit 'that this represents an entirely new contemporary type of German employer'.

existence of government and Reich. Dr. Schacht was the successful champion.

I spoke of German childhood from 'Weimar' to Dawes, that is to say, from the establishment of the constitution of the German body politic up to the life insurance of the German infant. That is what the Dawes plan means to the young Germany: life insurance. Without the Dawes plan it would have been impossible to maintain the political unity of Germany. Germany would have split asunder into its component parts, that is to say, would have been destroyed, dissolved into individual federal States, each having a currency of its own according to its economic basis.

And finally, after the embryonic period and after the infancy, the third and present phase of new Germany: adolescence, from the Dawes plan to Locarno and Geneva. That means, from the life insurance of Germany to the mutual life insurance of the European Powers based on the 'system of Locarno'. In other words, from national egotism to mutual understanding and supernational agreement, to a sort of international organization and co-operative society. That is the outstanding feature of the present phase of new Germany: the German initiative for this new order and system.

And the surprising and convincing expression of that fact is this: that such an international policy is represented and even guided—by whom ? By him who was and still is considered Germany's hero, by the former Field-Marshal and present President von Hindenburg, whereas those as far back as the second period who had the sagacity and courage to discern and strive for the same policy were assassinated or insulted to death: Erzberger as an 'international Catholic', Rathenau as an 'international Jew', and Ebert as an 'international Socialist'—each one being a good patriot gifted with vision and courage. There is good, sound historical sense in the idea of the new Germany of 1926 erecting a common monument on the Hohenstein to the memory of Ebert, Rathenau, and Erzberger, a monument to consist of nothing but one strong massive rock. This symbol of the martyrs of the young republic may well remind us of the words of Lichtenberg: 'To build up a republic with the materials of a shattered monarchy is a difficult problem. It cannot be done until each stone has been re-cut. And that takes time.'

What the infancy of new Germany failed to understand, the adolescence of the young Germany has learned to understand; and it has grasped the opportunity, beginning with a German constitution which expressly established the principle of reconciliation of the nations (Art. 118) and enshrining a German conviction which the nation is steadfastly purposed to fulfil.

I considered it necessary and advisable to describe and make clear these facts regarding the emergence of a new Germany out of the old Germany, as it is only upon the basis of such an association of ideas that those facts and problems become clear and intelligible and can be discussed and solved—the facts which are characteristic features of this new Germany and which we shall inquire into later on.

## II

THE young Germany of the new democracy, the Germany of the Weimar constitution, is after all really an old Germany, the Germany of my South German grandfather, of the South German Prince Max von Baden, the Germany of the men of 1848, the Germany of St. Paul's Church at Frankfort.

'In St. Paul's Church at Frankfort sat the assembly of the intellectual nobility of the German Nation. Never since then has a parliament been imbued with such noble sentiments for the welfare of mankind, with such moral uplift.'[1]

The French Revolution in February 1848, a radical proletarian revolution, extended into Germany, where it developed into a Liberal bourgeois upheaval. In the towns of south and central Germany the leaders of liberalism and of the idea of a unified Germany demanded liberal constitutions and the convocation of a German Parliament, and actually succeeded in obtaining them from their Governments. The Government of Baden demanded from the Federal Council the election of a German Parliament. King Frederick William of Prussia relented on the 18th of March, under the pressure of the barricades in the streets of Berlin. He even decked himself out with the black-red-and-gold colours, and issued a proclamation to the effect that 'Prussia in future will be dissolved into Germany'.— The Federal Council called upon the federal States to order the election of German national representatives by universal franchise. About 600 elected members assembled in St. Paul's Church at Frankfort on the 18th of May 1848

[1] Fritz Wuessing, *Geschichte des deutschen Volks.*

as the German National Assembly, and remained in session for one year, until, in consequence of the victory of the reactionaries of absolutism, first in Vienna, then in Berlin, several Governments recalled their representatives, and the Radical Left moved as a Rump Parliament to Stuttgart, where it was ultimately broken up by State troops. In the course of its deliberations the National Assembly split up into two parties: the Greater Germany party, which desired union with German Austria, and the Little German party, which wanted Prussia to be the leader. The idea was to have an hereditary Emperor at the head of the future German Federal State, who should share the responsibility of government with Federal ministers responsible to Parliament. The Assembly proposed a House of Commons elected by universal and equal franchise, and an Upper House composed of the ruling Princes and 161 elected members. Ultimately the King of Prussia was elected 'Emperor of the Germans' with 290 votes — the remaining 263 abstaining from voting. But the King of Prussia declined the imperial crown offered to him by a deputation, as he wished to reign by the grace of God, and not by the will of the people. He called the imperial crown offered to him 'an imaginary hoop made up of dirt and laths', and furthermore declared that 'the National Assembly only wanted to put a dog-collar round the neck of that fool, the King of Prussia, to bind him indissolubly to the sovereignty of the people, and make him the serf of the revolution....' Hence the unqualified negative to the deputation from St. Paul's Church and as a parting shot the plain truth: 'The only remedy against democrats is soldiers. Good morning!' In 1857 the mental disease with which the King was afflicted became so obvious that his brother William was entrusted with the Regency, the same who in 1871 became the Emperor William I. 'The work of the

St. Paul's Church Assembly was wrecked by the power and self-consciousness of the individual states, and by the lack of organization among the middle classes and the proletariat. But without the never-ceasing permeation of the people with the idea of national unity on a liberal basis Bismarck's work would have been immeasurably more difficult of accomplishment.' The Weimar National Assembly of 1919 gathered up the several threads of the ideals of the Frankfort National Assembly in 1848.

'Weimar' and 'Frankfort' belong together: Weimar, the town of Goethe and Schiller and Herder, of the *intelligentsia* and the humanism of the leading German classics— and Frankfort, the city of Goethe and Schopenhauer, of the *intelligentsia* and of the Europeanism of the first German Parliament of 1848.

What 'Frankfort' wanted and prepared in 1848, the democratic constitution of a unified Germany under the black, red, and gold flag, 'Weimar' carried out and completed in 1919 in the form of a democratic republic under the same historical flag.

Between 'Frankfort' and 'Weimar' lie sociologically the rise and growth of the fourth estate, the labouring class: its class organization and class consciousness. That is a new and essential addition made by 1919 to the policy of 1848.

Between 'Frankfort' and 'Weimar' lies, politically, the circuitous road via Potsdam–Berlin: the roundabout way via the Prussian monarchy of the Hohenzollerns, the exclusion of the Austria of the Habsburgs in 1866 from the German Confederation, and then the North German Federation of 1866—this roundabout way to a German Empire of 1871, which did not become a State of the German people, but an 'Everlasting Federation of Princes', under the supremacy of the Prussian crown, predominant in the German Federal Council.

## LECTURE II

A circuitous road, which historically appears to have been necessary, because through Bismarck it led to unification, although only a relative unification, without the German part of Austria, and involving the maintenance of twenty dynasties.

A circuitous road, which out of the German yearning for unity and liberty only led to this form of unity, but not to the liberty of democracy.

A circuitous road, finally, which led, by way of 1866 and 1870, to 1918 and 1919, that is to say, to 'Compiègne' and to 'Versailles', but also to 'Weimar', which, by way of 1870 and 1866, consciously extended back to 1848, and so added a new liberty to a new unity: in the constitution of the State of the people, which established the sovereignty of the people, a Government 'of the people, by the people, for the people'.

This constitution of the new Germany profited, it is true, by other democratic constitutions: from the English constitution in its prescriptive rights, from the two French constitutional laws in its parliamentarism, from the federal constitution of the United States in its federal organization, and from the Swiss Confederation in the matter of the referendum. But this Weimar constitution also has a conscious intellectual connexion with the Frankfort Parliament of 1848-9, the ideals of which have supplied most of the material for rearrangement and reconstruction. In order to show the similar spirit of 'Frankfort' and of 'Weimar' let me quote only the Preamble: 'This Constitution has been framed by the German People, united in its several parts, and animated by the desire to renew and to establish its Federation on the solid bases of liberty and justice, to serve the cause of peace both within and without, and to promote social progress.' The Constitution as a whole is governed by the following categorical sentences: 'The

German Federation is a Republic. Supreme Power emanates from the people. ... Every State must have a Republican Constitution. ... Each State Government requires the confidence of the State Parliament.' Resolutions of the Reichstag in favour of a change require the presence of two-thirds of the total membership and the support of two-thirds of those present.

Thus the German Constitution has set up, side by side with the three previously established types of republics, a new, a fourth form. The three chief types are: the president-republic (United States), the parliamentary republic (France), and the collective republic (Switzerland). The new Germany has the special form of a parliamentary democratic republic, having three chief centres of governmental authority: the President of the Reich, the Reichstag, and the Government of the Reich. For the sake of brevity and conciseness let me quote the summarized judgement of an English statesman on this new constitution. His Britannic Majesty's ambassador to Germany, Viscount d'Abernon, stated in a report (1919) to his Government:

Since the passage into force of the Weimar Constitution sovereign powers are vested by the German people in the Reichstag and the President of the Reich elected by universal suffrage. The President in turn appoints the Government, that is to say, the Chancellor and Ministers of the Reich, who must enjoy the confidence of the Reichstag during the exercise of their functions. ... The President of the Reich is vested with the usual formal prerogatives which belong to the constitutional head of a State with Parliamentary Government, but the declaration of war and conclusion of peace are effected by legislation in the Reichstag. He has the right to form the Government as well as to exercise supreme command over the armed forces. He exercises certain rights of control *vis-à-vis* the Reichstag by virtue of the powers vested in him by the Constitution. He does not possess the right of veto on legislation. ... Legislation dealing with foreign relations is, according to Art. 6 of the Constitution, the exclusive prerogative of the Reich. Similarly, Art. 78 ordains that the care and conduct of relations between the Reich and foreign States lies exclusively in the hands of the Reich. ... Art. 45 states that the President represents the Reich in international law. He accredits and receives diplomatic representatives. He concludes alliances and treaties with foreign States in the name of the Reich. His authority is limited in the sense that declaration of war or peace require legislation on the part of the Reichstag; similarly treaties involving legislation for their fulfilment require the assent of the Reichstag. His ordinances require for their validity the counter-signature of the Chancellor or of the competent Minister of the Reich. The practical conduct of foreign affairs lies in the hands of the Foreign Minister who controls the Executive and is directly responsible to the Reichstag. The Government are collectively entitled and obliged to lay down the general lines of foreign policy.

Let me add a few details, which one must be acquainted with, in order to be in a position to pronounce judgement upon this new Germany—now a composite, decentralized organism, neither unitary nor federal:

(1) With regard to the President. Any German man or woman over thirty-five years of age can be elected to the office of President. The period of office is seven years, re-election is permissible, and there is no limit to the number of re-elections. The election is by general, equal, direct, and secret ballot, by the vote of every German man and woman (married and unmarried) over twenty years of age. In case of a conflict between President and Parliament the people has the right of decision through a plebiscite.

(2) The Chancellor of the Reich. He is no longer Prussian Prime Minister, as was the Chancellor of the old Empire, and consequently he is also no longer dependent

upon the Prussian Diet, formerly the Conservative chamber of the plutocratic three-class electoral system which was the real supporting pillar of the policy and power of the German Empire. The Chancellor must now enjoy the confidence of the German Reichstag.

(3) The Reichstag (Parliament). This is elected by means of the same franchise as the President of the Reich, that is to say, by general, equal, direct, and secret ballot, by every man and woman, married or single, over twenty years of age. We have the proportional system, which enables every minority to have its representative in Parliament. Thus the candidates are not elected as persons, as individuals, but as representatives of programmes, of principles, of parties. One defect of this system is obvious: the lack of personal connexion between electors and elected, which on the other hand can be an advantage, because it ensures the independence of the elected in relation to the electors. Another drawback to proportional suffrage is that, in the event of the death of an elected member during the lifetime of a Parliament, the next candidate on the electoral list automatically moves up into his place; this excludes the possibility of by-elections, in which the political development of the will of the people might express itself as in a barometer.

Side by side with these three representative governmental authorities there is yet another, which is direct and immediate: that of the initiative of the people and the referendum.

Those three central authorities are the three unitary organs of the new Germany. Federal law over-rides local law. In addition, there is a federal organ: the Reichsrat, the Council of the Reich. This new Reichsrat no longer possesses the same importance as the old Bundesrat, the Federal Council. That organ of the several federal States was the real sovereign of the old Empire. It decided which Bills should be presented to the old Reichstag, and actually passed decisions upon the resolutions of the old Reichstag. It possessed the executive power. It was absolutely independent of the people's representatives, and in reality always had a Prussian majority. While the President of the Bundesrat was the Prussian Prime Minister, now the president of the Reichsrat is a delegate of the Reich. As distinguished from the old Bundesrat, first of all, Prussia has no special privileges in the new council, the Reichsrat. Secondly, the new Reichsrat has no prerogatives over the Reichstag, not even equality of rights with the Reichstag; and thirdly, the new Reichsrat is in no shape or form the sovereign power in the Reich. The new Reichsrat has merely certain rights of co-operation in legislative matters, and, moreover, very limited rights. It is true it has initiative rights in promoting legislation, and secondly it is entitled to be heard before Bills are presented to Parliament—but it has no right of rejection. Thirdly and lastly it certainly has the right to question legislation passed by the Reichstag; but this right is invalid and abortive in the face of a two-thirds majority of the Reichstag.

To this constitutional federal authority in the new Germany, to this Reichsrat, actual practice has added the occasional assembly of State Presidents. The grave decisions affecting foreign policy, with which the Government of the Reich repeatedly found itself confronted on account of the demands of the Allied and Associated Powers, emphasized the need of assuring and consolidating the authority of the Government of the Reich by inviting the State Presidents to Berlin, thoroughly acquainting them with the actual state of affairs, and in this way securing the assent of the State Presidents to the decisions of the Government of the Reich. The Reich always succeeded in doing so, mostly by a unanimous vote. This assembly of State Presidents is, however, only an occasional assembly, and its significance is merely of a tactical nature.

Let me add a few figures. This new Germany is composed of 18 'Länder', i.e. regions (formerly 25 States); these 18 regions have altogether 66 votes. Of this number Prussia has 26 in the Reichsrat (the Prussian Government 13, the twelve Prussian provinces one each, and the municipal district of Berlin one). The Prussian Government controls in fact no more than 13 votes, a fifth of the whole; the other 13, representing the provinces and Berlin, can vote against the Prussian Government. Bavaria has 10 votes, Saxony 7, Wurtemberg 4, Baden 3, Thuringia, Hessen, Hamburg 2 each, all other regions one vote each. Of the 63 millions of the German population 38 millions belong to Prussia (61 per cent.), Bavaria has 7·4 millions (12 per cent.), Saxony 5 millions, Wurtemberg 2·6 millions, Baden 2·3 millions, Thuringia 1·6 million, Hessen 1·3 million, and Hamburg 1·1 million. Prussia and Bavaria combined claim three-fourths of the population of Germany, whereas the remaining fourth is spread over the other 16 States of the Federation.[1] Those figures show the predominant importance of Prussia. But while in consequence of the unequal franchise and of the privileges of the House of Lords (Herrenhaus) the Prussia of old Germany was under

[1] The German population to-day (63 millions) is equal to that in 1908. In 1871 the population of Germany was 41 millions, in 1914, 68 millions; had there been no war and its aftermath the population of Germany to-day would be 75 millions. Of the 454 millions of people in Europe 100 millions (22 per cent.) belong to European Russia, 63 millions (14 per cent.) to Germany, 44 millions (9.7 per cent.) to Great Britain, 39 millions each (8·6 per cent. each) to France and Italy. The population of the European States increased by 10 per cent. within a century up to the middle of the eighteenth century, thence by 30 per cent. up to 1800, by 50 per cent. up to the development of the steam-engine and the railroads by 500 per cent. up to the World War.

## LECTURE II

the predominance of the 'Junkers', the Conservative landed proprietors (a type essentially different from the English Conservative), the new Prussia is a strongly democratic republic, in consequence of the universal franchise which brings out the social structure of Prussia. The new Prussia has been ruled by the 'coalition of Weimar', the co-operation of Democrats, Catholic Centre, and Socialists, from the very beginning of the new order up to the present time. The new Prussia is the corner-stone of the German republic, as the old Prussia was that of the military monarchy. The democratic development of the southern States was much more advanced than that of Prussia, especially that of my home country, Wurtemberg, and of the neighbouring State, Baden: as far back as a century ago they had solved political problems which still occupied and harassed Prussia during the war. That is why Baden was commonly called by public opinion a 'model commonwealth' and Wurtemberg was once called by the Emperor a 'monarchical republic'.

An institution which only exists in this new Germany, and nowhere else in the world, is the 'Reichswirtschaftsrat', a Federal Economic Council of the Reich. As its name implies, it is, together with the Works Councils Act (Betriebsrätegesetz) which replaces autocracy by democracy in the factories, an echo, a relic, of the Workmen's Council idea, the sole realization of all the demands of the Soviet Council system, such as began to make themselves heard during the first year of the revolution under the influence of the Russian Soviet State. The Economic Council is the representative of the individual professions: agriculture, industry, commerce, banking, traffic, transport, trades, consumers, officials, and the liberal professions ('freie Berufe'). It consists of 326 members all told, of which roughly 300 are nominated by the organizations and unions of those professions, and twelve each by the Government of the Reich and by the Council of the Reich respectively. It is the duty and the prerogative of this Economic Parliament to be heard as an expert in matters affecting economic and social policy. This Economic Parliament is being closely watched in foreign countries, but it has not been able to achieve very much in actual practice, because differences affecting economic interests are fought out in the Political Parliament. Also because the Reichstag as Political Parliament mostly ignored the expert activities of the Economic Parliament, by reason of certain objections of principle to anything in the form of a second parliament. Bismarck too had the intention of compensating the Reichstag by a Reichswirtschaftsrat (1880), but failed before the resistance of the Reichstag. On the other hand, in the very political sphere from which it was intended to exclude it, the Economic Parliament has done some really important and effective work, especially during the first years of unrest and during the inflation period, because as a sort of round table it established a certain personal human understanding between employers and employees, producers and consumers —in the first instance only physically, but afterwards also psychologically, because the need for mutual study of economic problems ultimately forced and educated both parties to come down to bedrock, to hard cast-iron facts.

And now we come to the parties in the Reichstag and the question of their part in the formation of the Government. The German Parliament, the Reichstag, is composed of 493 members, which at present are divided into nine parties. You will see that Germany is as yet a long way off from the two-party system, and probably always will be.

But first of all a few figures. Of the 493 members 36 are women, who are fairly equally divided among all parties,

## LECTURE II

with the exception of the 'Economic Party' (Wirtschaftspartei) and the 'Völkische Partei' (Supernationalists, Antisemites), in which there are no women members.

The figures relative to the various parties are as follows: the two extreme groups—(right) the 'Völkische' (Supernationalists) 14, and (left) the Communists 45; then the two great flanking parties—(right) the Nationalists (Deutsch-Nationale) 111, and (left) the Socialists (Sozialdemokratie) 131; then the parties of the middle (altogether 5)—Democrats 32, Catholic Centre 69, People's Party (Volkspartei) 51. These are really the three chief parties of the middle. Then there are two more groups: the Economic Party (a new group for the economic interests of the victims of inflation) with 21, and the Bavarian People's Party (a Bavarian Catholic party) with 19.

When one hears talk about the Reichstag and its party conditions, what is always most emphasized and objected to is the fact of its numerous, all too numerous, parties, and people are always longing for and demanding reduction and simplification. People then mostly point with a certain amount of envy to the English and American pattern of the two-party system. But such comparisons break down because they ignore fundamental differences in tradition and development.

The fact is incontrovertible and we have to face it, that Germany was the chief scene of the Reformation and of the Thirty Years War, and since then Germany has been divided into two sections, separated from each other denominationally: the Protestant Lutherans and the Catholics. Further, the fact remains that, through the socialist Karl Marx and through the dogmas of Marxism, Germany has been thoroughly imbued with the theory and practice of the class struggle. And finally the third fact remains, that the old Germany was not a uniform coherent State of the people, but a confederation of dynasties, several of which have clung to their particularism, not only in opposition to centralization but even to the idea of German unity.

These three historical facts in themselves have created three parties in Germany which in their particular form and in their essential importance are not to be found in any other nation : the Catholic Centre, the organization of the Catholic electorate; the Bavarian People's Party, the organization of the Bavarian (Catholic) Centre; and the Socialists, who, as distinguished from the Labour Party in other countries, had under the old régime assumed a class-war character and fought against and rejected the old State. You are doubtless aware that Bismarck's policy, his struggle against the 'Ultramontanism' and 'Romanism' of the Catholic Party, and his struggle against the 'Internationalism' of the Socialists, had historically their own share in the promotion and development of these persecuted opposition parties.

And then, after all, there is the historical fact that there has been since the Russian revolution a Russian propaganda for a revolution in Germany, which, in view of the immediate neighbourhood of a communistic Russia, particularly tended to develop the communistic movement in Germany.

Thus we are faced with the fact that there is really only a faint possibility of a reduction in, or a simplification of, those nine parties; a reduction really to eight only, provided the Bavarian Catholic Party is reunited as it formerly was with the German Catholic Centre Party; or perhaps at the utmost to seven, if the Democratic Party and the People's Party join hands and form a Democratic Liberal party—a development in which I personally have not much faith, because, notwithstanding the similarity in the political programmes of these two parties, their economic ideas and social interests are wide apart. The People's Party is synonymous with industry, with special emphasis on 'heavy' industry (iron and coal works), and the Democratic Party is representative of the middle classes, and the *intelligentsia*, &c.

You see, therefore, that a two-party system with a clean division into Right and Left is out the question. Nevertheless, in spite of the apparent ramifications of these nine parties, there are in the end only three possible coalitions, all three of which have one thing in common, namely, the fact that the concentration of forces lies neither on the right nor on the left, but in the middle.

These three possibilities are:

(1) The 'Small Coalition'—of the middle parties: Democrats plus Catholic Centre plus People's Party. This may be tolerated or supported from the Right by the Nationalists, a coalition which prepared Locarno—a coalition which Stresemann wittingly brought together for the purpose of Locarno, in order, as he once said to me, 'to lead the Nationalists through the purgatory of responsibility'. In this leadership he was successful, it is true, only up to the gates of Locarno, but not into the 'purgatory' of Locarno. Or there is another possibility: tolerance and support from the left by the Socialists, as was the case last winter during the great unemployment crisis, the worst period of unemployment which Germany has ever experienced. There were two million unemployed. That means, in round figures, ten million human beings compelled to live on support from the State—that is to say, 16 per cent. of the German people.

(2) The 'Great Coalition'—of all Constitutional parties from the Socialists by way of the Democrats and the Catholic Centre up to the People's Party; excluding the extreme groups on the left and on the right, the Communists and

Nationalists, while they are anti-state, anti-republican. The former Socialists are to-day Conservatives and the former Conservatives are to-day Revolutionaries.

(3) The 'Weimar Coalition' of the three republican parties of the Weimar period: Socialists, Democrats, and Catholic Centre, who jointly decided upon and adopted the Weimar constitution. I said 'of the Weimar period', because since then the parties which accept the Republic have been increased by the People's Party, the Bavarian Catholic Party, and the Economic Party.[1]

All these three possible combinations have, I repeat, always one thing in common, namely, the permanent concentration of forces in the middle and centre. That results in and explains the stability of the foreign policy of the new Germany. Whereas in home policy the economic problems and the problems of unitarism (not to be confused with centralism), discussions about the new flag, and with the former ruling princes, created unrest, there is an unmistakable stability in foreign policy dating from the association of Wirth and Rathenau as Chancellor and Foreign Secretary under President Ebert and leading up to the Dawes agreement, Locarno, and Geneva. This stability in the foreign policy of the new Germany is all the more striking when we remember the 'zigzag course' of the old Germany.

The personality of the German Minister of Foreign Affairs, Dr. Stresemann, is typical of the new Germany; he is the manifest embodiment of the development during the last few years. Stresemann was the man who, as founder and leader of the People's Party, himself bred and trained

[1] And now (January 1927) finally even by the Nationalists (Monarchists): they have now recognized the constitution of Weimar, the republic, the new flag, and the international policy of Locarno and Geneva, and are supporting this new Germany.

all the opposition against which he, at a later stage, as minister and statesman, had to fight, and which he has now surmounted at last. No matter whether it was the flag question, the republic, or the 'policy of fulfilment', the People's Party was negative so long as it had not to bear a share of the burden of responsibility. It became increasingly positive with increased responsibility. Stresemann started as a party leader, became an educator of his party, and is now a statesman. He has evolved from his old opportunism, under the experience of responsibility, to a new conception of Germany's part in world politics, because he has the gift of a creative intuition. He appears to be indispensable to every German cabinet, became Minister for Foreign Affairs again and again, after every crisis, and is likely to remain so. In this respect Stresemann, who has been a minister in six cabinets, resembles his French contemporary Briand, who has been minister in ten, for whom the spirit of Locarno has a feature of mysticism. The historical importance of Stresemann will possibly prove to lie in the fact that it was he who recovered and secured for Germany her freedom of action in foreign policy. In this sense he deserves, side by side with the historic Bismarck of Unity, the title of the 'Bismarck of Liberty'. Dr. Stresemann was, and is, qualified for the work not only by his intelligence but also by his courage. It is significant that Stresemann can deliver in the University of Heidelberg an address about 'Goethe and the wars of Liberation'. General Dawes and Mr. Owen D. Young told me in America that Stresemann is one of the most courageous statesmen they know. About Dr. Schacht, President of the Reichsbank, they expressed the same judgement, based upon their personal experiences.

Such statesmanship reminds me of what a biographer said regarding Freiherr vom Stein: 'It may need intelligence to be a brilliant talker or a clever writer; but greater intelligence is needed to have a right understanding of realities, to penetrate behind the confusing foreground of day-to-day events to the background where the future is to be discerned; and the greatest of intellectual achievements is to have both a right vision of realities and a creative power to call this reality into being in face of every temporary resistance.'

That unmistakable stability in foreign policy appears to me to be an effective retort to the talk about the 'crisis in democracy and parliamentarism'. We are passing through a crisis, but only a crisis of technicalities, of the technique of parliamentarism, not of the democratic idea. We have as yet to grapple with the task of developing the technique of parliamentarism, which is a new and immature thing so far as we are concerned. The so-called crisis in German democracy is rather more in the nature of literary criticism than a political crisis. Hard facts have refuted the catchword about the economic 'expert', who posed as a political leader, and the Stinnes catastrophe has opened the eyes of even those people who do not know the difference between economic and political reasoning. Recent developments have refuted the catchword about a 'dictator'. Marshal Hindenburg, the man nominated as candidate for the Presidency by certain people, some of whom thought of him, wanted him, as 'militarist' or 'monarchist' and as 'dictator', has developed, within the lines of political expediency, into a moral leader of a democratic, republican, and peaceful Germany, of the Germany of international co-operation. It is ever and always the same, realities and responsibility are the best educators. We know what Kant said: 'One cannot ripen into freedom, if one has not first been freed. The first attempts, to be sure, will be crude, generally also accompanied by an oppressive and dangerous state of affairs, but we cannot develop reason except by our own endeavours and responsibility.'

The best example of education in responsibility by facts is Hindenburg himself. The most representative general of the monarchical army takes the oath to the republican constitution. That means that the idea of the unity of the people has triumphed over monarchical legitimacy. Hindenburg's political attitude since then could only surprise those who knew nothing about, or failed to appreciate, the outstanding facts in his previous attitude.

(1) Who advised the German Emperor to leave Germany? Hindenburg, on the 8th of November 1918, the first day of the revolution. And why? To do what Abraham Lincoln did for the United States: to save the unity of the nation.

(2) Who was the first to place himself at the disposal of Ebert, at that time not yet President, but a workmen's leader, a 'revolutionary'? Hindenburg, on the 9th of November 1918, the second day of the revolution. And why? To save the union of the German nation.

(3) Who advised the German Government and its representative, Erzberger, to accept the terms of the Armistice? Hindenburg. And why? To save the union of the German nation.

(4) Who was the first to intervene publicly in favour of Walther Rathenau, when he was murdered, and why? Hindenburg—to save the union of the German nation.

That was the policy of the Field-Marshal. What was and is the policy of the President, and how did it proclaim itself?

(1) From the very first moment, in his exchanging the military uniform for the frock coat of the civilian. That symbol means more in Germany than elsewhere.

(2) By his excluding from his immediate entourage in

Berlin all those nationalistic friends who surrounded him at Hanover.

(3) By his retaining and confirming in office the same Chancellor (Dr. Luther), the same Foreign Minister (Dr. Stresemann), the same chief of his Secretariat (Dr. Meissner), who had been the advisers of Ebert.

And (4) by specially, in his first proclamation addressed to the German people, praising President Ebert as a national figure, a meritorious patriot, though the Nationalists had just insulted him as an 'international traitor' to Germany.

And all this, not by any means for reasons of 'opportunism', nor of 'senility', as, strange to say, we now sometimes hear the very people whispering, for whom a year ago he was so far from senile that they could nominate him as a candidate for the Presidency (by the way, a certain Marshal Foch is of about the same age, and still engaged in active work); Hindenburg the general and Hindenburg the President had, and have, one and the same object in view: service to the people, to give the people a one hundred per cent. service. Hindenburg is like the American General Washington, first in war, first in peace. The erection of a national monument in honour of those who were victims of the war is now under consideration in Germany. What is the suggestion of Hindenburg? Not to erect a war monument for warriors, but to change a military guard-house in Berlin into a chapel dedicated to the memory of our lost and loved and to faith and peace. Hindenburg has nothing in common with MacMahon, who endangered the French Republic in its seventh year. The German Republic is in its seventh year stronger than the French was. Hindenburg is not a Dictator and he does not want to be one. Germany is as far from Mussolinism as from Russian Leninism. Hindenburg embodies a striking example of education in democracy by responsibility, both in himself, and in his work for the German people. Hindenburg stabilizes the republic by his example; he is the symbol of responsibility.

It was the historic mission of the first President, Ebert, to win over the labouring classes to the new State; it will be the historic mission of the second President, Hindenburg, to win over the bourgeoisie to the new republic. Both together saved the German union, and each one served, one after the other, the German Republic.

Monarchy has collapsed, and the collapse is final. The monarchy lasted for a little less than forty-eight years, not even two complete generations, and had only two monarchs, William I and his grandson William II; between the two, Frederick reigned for a brief ninety-eight days. Their Germany was an 'Everlasting Federation of Princes'. It had not only one Monarch in Chief, but twenty-two local kings and princes. This fact, while being a cause of weakness in the old Germany, is to the new Germany a source of security against monarchy. Monarchy can never return, because its rehabilitation is not focused on one particular person, but on many. Only in one State of the German Republic does the attitude of mind of the majority seem to be leaning towards a monarchy. Prince Rupprecht of Bavaria would seem to have a majority of sympathizers in Bavaria, but only in his own native State. But the German Constitution definitely precludes his reinstatement. Such an occurrence is out of the question, just as it would be according to the American Constitution, where one single American State cannot become a monarchy in the midst of the American Commonwealth. Furthermore, the Bavarian prince being a Catholic, Germany as a whole, because of her Protestant majority, would never accept a Catholic prince as sole monarch. Prince Rupprecht personally, by the way, is far too intelligent not to be aware of all this. In fact, he has repeatedly and publicly declined to place himself at the disposal of those desiring a restoration of the monarchy. If the monarchists were called upon to-day to occupy the throne, they would find themselves in a very difficult position, because they have no candidate. The former Emperor has been forgotten in Germany more quickly than abroad. The popular romance of imperial heroism and prestige has disappeared from a nation from which the Emperor himself has disappeared. This indeed was the best he could do, for his departure averted civil war and saved German union. The hardest blow to the monarchy has been struck by the monarchs themselves, in demanding very large compensation from the impoverished people.

Education by facts and responsibility to a new spirit is a characteristic feature of the majority in the new Germany, among leaders and among the people. Let me pick out just one profession, the education of which from monarchical-military reasoning to democratic, even pacifist, conviction is more surprising and more significant than any other.

The attitude of mind and the spirit of responsibility that you have seen in Hindenburg you will find in other former generals of high intellectual standing (I emphasize the intellectual standing). As an example I may cite General von Seeckt, the late chief of the 'Reichswehr', often spoken of, but really known by few. I remember well the nights I spent in his company during the time of the nationalist 'Kapp-Putsch'. His judgement was more severe, and he was willing to act more sternly against the rebel general, his former comrade in arms, than the civilian Government: he wanted him court-martialled. The loyal co-operation of President Ebert and General von Seeckt saved the republic several times.

Generals such as von Deimling, von Schoenaich, Count Montgelas, coming from the aristocracy, formerly famous as military chiefs, are now not only republican, but even leaders of the peace movement. For years they have been travelling all over Germany, speaking and writing articles, and educating the German people to international co-operation and intellectual disarmament. These military men are not militarists, simply because they were military men. They know the needs of a military system, and they also know that Germany really is disarmed. They have put their faith in peace and not in militarism: they are developing a science of peace instead of a science of war: they are substituting welfare for warfare.

The titles of the books written by these leading generals and officers are very significant:

General von Schoenaich: *Intellectual Disarmament; From Chaos to Reconstruction; The War in 1930; My Damascus.*

General von Deimling: *Gas Warfare of the Future; For the League of Nations.*

Fritz von Unruh: *Fatherland and Liberty; Speeches dedicated to the Resolute Fighters for the German Republic and for Peace for Humanity; The Pinions of Nike.*

Colonel Schützinger: *The Collapse; The Fight for the Republic.*

Colonel Franz Carl Endres: *The Tragedy of Germany; Reichswehr and Democracy; Fatherland and Humanity; Europe our Fatherland.*

And so on. *My Damascus*[1] (i. e. 'my conversion') seems to me to be a most characteristic title; likewise *Europe our Fatherland*.

Those of you to-day who are able to visit and inspect

[1] Verlag der Neuen Gesellschaft, Berlin.

the former great arsenal of Krupp in Essen, and all the German shipyards, will find that no war material is being manufactured there, but instruments of peace for scientific and economic purposes, from the instruments of the surgeon to agricultural machinery, and you will also see realized for the new Germany what the prophet foretold of old: 'They shall beat their swords into ploughshares and their spears into pruning-hooks.'

Now let me quote another instance from the new Germany, a fact concerning the working classes. I well remember the celebration of Constitution Day on the 11th of August 1925, when I heard the Prussian Minister of the Interior, Severing, a Socialist, prophesy that the economic crisis of the winter would be unavoidable as a consequence of inflation and deflation, and of lack of capital; he promised every effort to make the working classes understand the necessity of their weathering the crisis without political disturbances. Now have you heard of any such political disturbances? No!—This attitude of the working classes is an expression of their sense of responsibility under the most adverse circumstances, with two millions of unemployed.

What do these facts show? They show that the German Nation has become political. Moreover, the fact that 77 to 79 per cent. of the German people take part in the parliamentary elections is a proof of the political interest inherent in democratic Germany.

One so often hears, in Germany and out of it, that the German nation is 'unpolitical'. In this generalized form the statement is incorrect. It is true that the German nation has no such unerring political instinct as has the English, thanks to a tradition centuries old and experience gained by political responsibility. But it is equally true that the German nation has passed through political periods, has had political personalities and ideas, as rich and intensive as those of other nations.

Take the period of a hundred years ago—the philosophers of political democracy, and even of cosmopolitan ideas, Kant and Fichte; the leaders of South German democracy, Rotteck and Welcker; in the north, Stein and Hardenberg, who emancipated the peasants and democratized the municipal substructure of the State; Scharnhorst and Gneisenau, who democratized the social composition of the army; Wilhelm von Humboldt, representing the expression of liberal vital energy.

Then 1848—St. Paul's Church in Frankfort, an assembly of political heads of the first order, who reasoned constructively from the rights of man to everyday economic questions.

And even after 1870, during the first decade of the new Empire—Miquel, Bennigsen, and Lasker, Forckenbeck, Windhorst, and others.

But after that begins the political decline of the German nation. The majority of the nation ceased to be interested in politics, owing to universal economic prosperity and to Bismarck's national successes in the sphere of foreign policy, side by side with a Reichstag invested with no rights whatever except the right to talk, and which consequently gradually came to be called a 'Chatterbox', 'Talk-Shop', or 'Repetition Hall', with plenty of parleying but no sign of a Parliament. A radical member characterized this Reichstag as 'a mere fig-leaf to cover the nakedness of absolutism'. People of intellectual standing, therefore, who desired to take an active interest in affairs, turned to economics or science; politics became a business, a job to be attended to by the administration, by the bureaucracy. Even General Ludendorff at a later date admits in his *War Reminiscences*: 'The road travelled by our internal development contained no room for the expansion of personalities. Leading men in public life followed their profession and kept themselves aloof. There may have been able men in the Reichstag, capable of directing the fortunes of the country, but with the existing party system it was out of the question for them to come to the front. We were poor in prominent men. Our political system failed to produce new creative forces. It has pronounced judgement upon itself by its own sterility.' Ludendorff is quite right in denouncing the 'sterility of our political system', but he is wrong in accusing 'the existing party system'. Not the party system of a Reichstag which had no power at all was the real cause, but the old bureaucratic constitution and the absence of political responsibility. Even good government is no substitute for self-government.

The people trusted and worked, and the ordinary middle-class civilian population lived on in the spirit of Treitschke's head master, who proved to his own satisfaction that the Hohenzollern monarchy was the most suitable form of organization for the German people; and so, without venturing to criticize, and with implicit faith, the nation glided or stumbled into the world war. And it is this world war which becomes the educator in politics and democracy, through disillusion, distress, collapse.

A knowledge of the inner causes of events and their development is felt as a necessity, and the consequence is a Parliamentary Committee of Investigation and the publication of the secret archives, according to Clausewitz's historic demand, 'to tell the truth, the whole truth, and nothing but the truth'. The Parliamentary Committee of Investigation was first of all a consequence of defeat, and the outcome of the desire and need to inquire and find out how and why everything came about as it did. It developed more and more into a politico-scientific investigation of all problems connected with the war. It subdivided itself into four sub-committees: (1) For the investigation of the historical facts preceding the war, as far back as the policy of the Government of the Reich at the Hague Conferences. (2) For the investigation of the possibilities of peace during the war. (3) For the investigation of infractions of international law during the war. (4) For the investigation of the circumstances attending the German collapse. These committees include expert members of all parties, as well as scientific experts of every shade of opinion. I myself am a member. They have the right to study all secret archives and to take evidence from everybody. Thus, for instance, we have taken evidence from, among others, Hindenburg and Ludendorff, Bethmann-Hollweg, Helfferich, Kühlmann, and other generals and diplomats, confronting them with each other for several days at a time. The results are: the cleansing of parties from catchwords and prejudices, purifying public opinion from the poison with which it was infected, and education of the masses to think politically. The last document issued by the Committee concludes that the real decisive value of these investigations and interrogations is 'that contemporaries of the world war, who occupied leading positions, set down their recollections in black and white with a full sense of their responsibility, and gave reasons for the attitude adopted by them during the war. In this way the world of to-day, comparing evidence with counter-evidence, is supplied with the best conceivable material for forming its own judgement. Posterity, moreover, will in this evidence possess a practically priceless source of information for future study.' The inquiry into the Hague Conferences, especially, brought to light much new material upon which independent work has been done by authorities as diverse in their views as Dr. Wehberg the pacifist, Dr. Kriege the legal adviser of Imperial Germany, and General Count Montgelas. Just as we Germans had to change our views on the German attitude at the Hague (1899 and 1907) as a result of the opening of the archives and of the cross-examination of the ex-delegates, so general public opinion outside Germany will change as a consequence of the publication of the minutes of the protocol when these shortly see the light.

The publications issued by this Committee of Investigation are supplementary to, and a continuation of, the documents of the Foreign Office, the publication of which is also a consequence of defeat in the war. They range from 1871 (from the Peace of Frankfort) to 1914 (the assassination at Sarajevo) and comprise fifty-two volumes. Their importance in connexion with an understanding of the political history of the last two generations, and also the political education of the rising generation, is unrivalled. Never before in the history of the world has it been possible within such a short time after a war to learn so thoroughly and comprehensively all about the external and internal reasons and causes which led up to the catastrophe. Formerly the custom was to study documents when the actors whom they concerned were dead and buried. The German example presented to the world may prove a salutary lesson bearing good fruit, not only for Germany but for the whole world.

The problem of the political education of the masses raises the question of the selection of leaders. The old Germany was a bureaucracy, a State of officialdom, but not a State that selected the fittest of those born to be leaders. The new Germany chooses its leaders more democratically, by the co-operation of men in politics and in Parliament, and by proof of character and ability. Not one of the present leading men in the new Germany would have had the slightest chance of attaining a leading political position in the old Germany. None of them comes from the old Prussian aristocracy, all of them emanate from the Liberal bourgeoisie and the labouring classes. New men control a new machine. Such are, in the Reich: Stresemann (former secretary of an industrial organization), Schacht (President of the Reichsbank, former banker), Simons (President of the Supreme Court, former lawyer), Rathenau (former industrialist), Wirth (former teacher), Preuss (the author of the new Constitution, former teacher), Loebe (President of the Reichstag, former printer); and, in Prussia: Dr. Becker (Minister for Education, former teacher), Braun (Prime Minister, former agricultural labourer), Severing (Minister of Home Office, former locksmith). All are leaders by character and capacity, almost all are between forty and fifty years old. Neither Ebert nor Hindenburg would have had any political chance in the old Germany.

That is the point at which even the critics of democracy are compelled to acknowledge the advantages of the democratic system and technique. Even an advocate of Prussian nationalism like Oswald Spengler, who starts out from the statement that democracy has grown 'old and satiated', knows of nothing but democratic suggestions for his reconstruction of the German Reich, when it comes to the decisive problem of the selection of leaders. On the one hand the idea is to let a trained professional bureaucracy relieve the professional politicians of the actual office work of carrying on the government of the country, but on the other hand 'the object we have to aim at is, that a telegraph messenger may in three years' time stand a chance of becoming a Secretary of State, that every young man may feel the pressure of the marshal's baton in his knapsack'. Indeed, Spengler demands 'examination by the State, open to all, irrespective of age, sex, position, or early education'. What is this but democratic selection?

A special institution has been established in the new Germany for the purpose of the political education of leaders and people: the School of Politics in Berlin (Deutsche Hochschule für Politik).[1] I founded it for the new Germany, for the new generation, the generation of my son, type of the Young Germany, from whose fate I wanted to save his generation. I am convinced that politics needs the same application of scientific method which has developed economics and industry to their marvellous prosperity. You have schools for natural science, for technical engineering, for business administration, law schools and medical schools; why not political schools, for political administration, for human engineering? We demand efficiency from economics; why not demand efficiency from politics, and therefore training for politics? Politics touches not only the pocket but the life of the individual as well as of the nation. Rational control of emotional and instinctive impulses as well as application of the scientific spirit to human affairs must develop and improve world policy.

We started in 1920—we, that is to say, a group of practical men and scholars, such as: Dr. Simons (President of the Supreme Court of the Reich), Dr. Schacht (President of the Reichsbank), Dr. Preuss (the author of the new Constitution), Walther Rathenau, Dr. Drews (President of the Supreme Court for Government and Municipal Affairs), Dr. Becker, Dr. Meissner (Chief of Secretariat under Presidents Ebert and von Hindenburg), &c., and professors such as Meinecke, Delbrück, Troeltsch, Bonn, Schücking, von Schulze-Gaevernitz, and others, including also the leader of the German Women's Movement, Gertrud Bäumer, and other persons drawn from every party acknowledging the

[1] Berlin, Schinkelplatz 6.

new State: from the German People's Party to the Social Democrats, from Ebert to Stresemann, with the exception of the extreme Nationalists and Communists. With these two exceptions all parties are represented on the governing body; for example, men like Dr. Marx, the Chancellor of the Reich, and Braun, Prime Minister of Prussia. Most of the men named above are also actual teachers in our institute: Dr. Simons, the President of the Supreme Court of the Reich, comes to Berlin from Leipzig every Monday to lecture. Dr. Schacht, the President of the Reichsbank, and, formerly, Walther Rathenau, Dr. Preuss, and Dr. Stresemann, have lectured out of the fullness of their practical experience. The students of our institute include the more advanced students of the Berlin University, seeking further study in political science in addition to their University course, as well as officials of the Reich, the individual State municipal officials, young diplomats, officers, teachers, editors, workmen, secretaries, and leaders of political and economic organizations. We had 700 last winter and 550 last summer, and 1,200 during the winter term 1926–7, of whom approximately 10 per cent. were non-Germans. We are organized in half-yearly terms, like the University, and in lectures and seminars. In addition to the general course, which is mapped out to cover two years, at the end of which there is a diploma recognized by the State, there are special courses: for the younger diplomats, a course which the Foreign Office has made obligatory; for social and political officials of the new State; for editors; for leaders of organizations; for the youth-movement, and so on. The late Minister of the Interior in the Reich (Dr. Külz) ordered in 1926 that for officials of administration certificates of attendance at the School of Politics or certificates recording the passing of final examinations should be kept in the files and with the records of each officer, and he also recommended the Prussian Ministers of the Interior, of Justice, and of Education to issue similar orders. And whereas our central office in Berlin largely relies on the individual type of leader, our courses throughout the Reich reach the people outside: courses of one or two weeks each, with one problem in foreign or home policy each day, and an audience comprising all sections and grades of the people, from the president of a provincial government or the bishop to the working man and the promising high-school boy. Our first task was a national one: 'At the back of all my thoughts there is one thing: Germany.' These words of that genius Friedrich List, I inscribed upon the Deed of Foundation. Germany: that means the new Germany of the democratic republic. We might also add the democratic words of Freiherr vom Stein: 'National union implies love for the constitution, the right state of public opinion on national affairs and the ability of the citizens to manage affairs.' To educate the German citizen in such a spirit is all the more necessary if democracy means responsibility. For us democracy means not only a system, but a mentality: a system giving the people the privilege of selecting the fittest leader to serve the community; a mentality taking this privilege as an obligation towards the community. Consequently democracy implies responsibility of the people towards the community, not towards any class or caste, and responsibility of the leaders, not towards the people or any party, but towards the community. In other words, not to put an ear to the ground, not to follow public opinion, but to lead the nation, to have a vision of the future, and to have a courage for the present time.

The more the new State became consolidated, the more we were able to devote ourselves to our international aim: the promotion of an understanding of the need of international co-operation. It is our intention and our will to achieve the creation of a kind of 'aristocracies of democracies'. That we are on the right road is proved by such facts as that the Carnegie Foundation has selected our School of Politics for its German head-quarters and established a Carnegie Chair there; that we have entered into close relations with the League of Nations Institute of Intellectual Co-operation in Paris; and that the Geneva School for International Studies has established a system of co-operation with us. One of the most interesting and fruitful endeavours is our Juvenile Seminar, an association of the leaders of all organizations for youth—from Nationalists to Communists—which was inaugurated in the winter of 1925–6. Here, under the personal responsibility of young people of every shade of political opinion, political questions are dealt with by lecture and discussion, without even the most diametrically opposed views ever disturbing the businesslike and dispassionate discussion of the matter: a proof that the work of the institute is gradually—and that is surely no trifling result—strengthening the sense and feeling for moderation and decency in politics.

Just a few words on the subject of the Youth Movement in Germany—75 organizations with three million members. Germany has had Youth Movements before. There were three between 1813 and 1848, the generation of the Wars of Liberation, the Young Germany of the generation about 1835 (related to the European movement of Young Europe, as Mazzini called it), and the movement of 1848. Then there were no more movements between 1850 and 1880. There was no revival until in the 'eighties came naturalism in art (Gerhart Hauptmann), socialism in politics, and criticism in culture (Nietzsche). All this was in the nature of a protest against materialism in civilization and a prelude to the crisis which came to a head and exploded in the world war. No wonder that, after the world war, in a world which had been unable to prevent such a catastrophe, the disinclination to have anything to do with materialism and rationalism became stronger and more absolute than ever in the rising generation. 'The essence of every youth movement is the protest of human nature against the constraint of any kind of rigid, torpid, lifeless organization; the revolt of the soul against purely mechanical things, or the revolt of nature against civilization, or, to put it plainly, the revolt of the forces of life against forms inimical to life, the revolt of the personal and human against the material.'[1] The rising generation has a presentiment of this clean break, which is involved by the world war, a break such as has only once before been experienced with such tremendous force by mankind, the break between antiquity and Christianity. Thus a new rhythm, a cosmic lawfully ordered state of affairs is felt, sought, and found. 'In its realization of this spirit the German Youth Movement will prove to be more than a mere movement among people of a certain age. It is a beginning, and will extend and spread with and through the people, increasing year by year. As a powerful educational factor such as has never before been witnessed in our history, as a natural reaction of the soul against the dangers of our material civilization, the Youth Movement may take satisfaction in the fact that it is in close communion with the greatest and most

---

[1] So also Gertrud Bäumer, who points out that echoes of all motives of every present-day youth movement are already to be found in the writings of Goethe as a young man, and are expressed almost in the same words in various passages throughout his works. And furthermore that the same thought which the prophetic sense of Schiller opposed to the new world of civilization more than 100 years ago is lively to-day in the mass of the people. (See Schiller's *Letters on the Aesthetic Education of Mankind*).

decisive movements of our German past, with the movements which most faithfully reflect the true spirit of Germany. To live by and draw sustenance from these sources whence flows this spirit of Germany, that will be the object for it to aim at, and upon its success or failure to achieve this object will depend whether this movement is destined to fulfil its great mission, which is to make its influence felt decisively in the great contest between humanism and materialism.'

Whilst acknowledging the historical and actual necessity for the democratic parliamentary State, it is still possible, of course, to offer criticism with respect to certain regulations, institutions, and customs; suggestions may be made, for instance, for reforms in respect of the prerogatives of the President and of the Government, or for a reform of the franchise (smaller electoral districts, adult suffrage). These are questions of domestic policy.

Now we will consider and discuss the facts and problems of the international policy of Germany. That means passing from the written constitution to an inner conviction, from the calculation of the head to the appreciation of the heart and to international practice.

# III

WE have seen how the new Germany came into being and grew; we have considered its body, the constitution; and it now remains for us to show the convictions and aspirations of this new Germany.

It is our conviction that the road travelled by Germany is historically clear, and in a certain sense was a line of law, of necessity; also that the new Germany is the embodiment and the symbol not only of a German destiny of her own, but also of a joint European destiny. We know to-day that the road which led to Versailles and to Weimar was not merely the consequence of a military defeat, but that, together with other causes, this military defeat is also the outcome of political incompleteness, of spiritual isolation, of a political anachronism.

1848 marks the first turning in the road: away from a people's State with a German Emperor, elected by the will of the people.

1862–6 marks the second turning in the road: away from a united German State.

1871 creates a lesser Germany in the form of a larger Prussia, whose King wants to remain Emperor by the grace of God, whose Prussian Diet—undemocratic, unliberal, unsocial—has more influence in the Reich than the Reichstag.

This road was historically necessary, so long as it was the road of superior forces; it became unhistorical and dangerous as soon as it ignored the social remodelling of Germany and extended into the twentieth century, thus isolating Germany.

It is probable that an Emperor like Emperor Frederick—between William I and William II—would have had not only the discernment,[1] but the determination, for democratic reform. The programme of Crown Prince Frederick (1867 and 1870) was the establishment of the democratic constitution of the Liberal Parliament of Frankfort, 1848: to bring about the union of Germany, to merge Prussia in Germany, to change the federal States into a real Reich, a commonwealth of one State under the Hohenzollerns, to mediatize[2] all other kings and princes, depriving them of their sovereignty, allowing them titles but no power, to establish ministries of the Reich, responsible to the Reichstag—in a word, the parliamentary system, proposed by the National Assembly Frankfort 1848 as a democratic monarchy, and achieved by the National Assembly of Weimar 1919 as a democratic republic.

But Frederick's days were numbered, and with him the entire generation of German Liberalism dropped out of the running. He is the ninety-eight days' Emperor of 1888, the one who coined the saying about Bismarck's constitution:

[1] Compare what Crown Prince Frederick noted in his diary after the Franco-German War, 1870-1: 'At the moment it would seem as though we were neither loved nor respected, but simply feared. Other nations regard us as capable of every wickedness. Mistrust of us is increasing more and more. This is not simply the result of this war, it is first and foremost the result of the theory of blood and iron, discovered by Bismarck, constantly paraded in recent years. What good to us is all this power and victorious glory and clamour if hatred and mistrust confront us everywhere on our path. Bismarck has made us great and powerful, but he is robbing us of our friends, of the sympathies of the world, and of our own conscience. I still stand firmly to-day by the opinion that Germany could make moral conquests and become united, free, and powerful, without blood and iron, with the sole help of her own good right. How difficult will it be to fight against the blind worship of crude force and material success and to raise men's spirits again to direct their ambition and energies towards beautiful and wholesome ends!'

[2] This expression refers to the system under which the sovereign princes (kings, grand dukes, &c.) had an immediate relationship with the Emperor, a relic of medieval feudalism and of the Holy Roman Empire, peculiar to Germany.

'artificial chaos'. He was a personality full of sympathy for the constitution of the country of his English consort.

But the old Germany remained a Germany of two nations: one, the rising generation of the labouring classes, inimically disposed towards the State and declining to have anything to do with it, called by the Emperor William II 'a traitorous rabble' or 'fellows without fatherland'; the other, the liberal-minded bourgeoisie, whose attitude towards the State was that of indifference, lacking all sense of co-operation, of responsibility, the undiscriminating *Untertan*[1] (subject or citizen), saturated with national successes, prosperous, and living in an atmosphere of vacuous adoration of a State based upon might.

But it was a wrong track from the national as well as the international point of view: the ideology of Might was the wrong trail for the whole of Europe and the whole world as well. This 'Realpolitik', this 'realistic policy', led to that mechanism of alliances and armaments, to that complicated machinery of suspicion and competition, the strain and overstrain of which burst and exploded in nationalism and imperialism, and finally in world war. I may in this connexion remind you of the judgements of Presidents Wilson and Coolidge, already quoted. (Lord Grey too has stated that 'the root cause of the world war was the division of Europe into groups of Powers with competing armaments'.)

The new Germany of to-day knows the historical inevitableness of this development. The new Germany believes that she is able to understand the true inward meaning of the old paths. We now believe and know that the world war was only a part, only one form of expression

[1] Title of a topical novel by Heinrich Mann, describing this type of German citizen at the beginning of the twentieth century.

## LECTURE III

of a world-wide upheaval, which we are able to comprehend cosmically. During the last few decades, in every sphere of life we see a revolution of the mind, seeking and finding a new form of expression, of rhythm. We see it in literature and art, painting and music; in natural science, Einstein's relativity; in psychology, Freud's psycho-analysis; in philosophy, Count Keyserling's universalism; in religion, the cosmic interdependence. The fashioning of social, economic, national, and political affairs plays its own special part in this new spiritual readjustment. For us the world war is also an outward expression of this inward upheaval, albeit the most drastic, the most cruel expression, but precisely for this reason palpable and salutary. For my own part, I am convinced that the period around and about the world war represents a tremendous break in the ordinary course of the history of mankind, a metamorphosis such as has occurred only once before, namely, in the break between the ancient times and Christianity. There can therefore be no such thing as going back for this new Germany, no repairing, no restoration, no re-establishment, no re-constitution, either of the old Germany or of the old world. That was and is for us a sort of antediluvian period. We know what the saying means: 'Let the dead bury their dead.' We want the watchword to be what Goethe expressed: 'Die and rise again!'

For us there is one thing and one only: a new birth, a new rhythm, a creative order not only of a new Germany, but also of a new world. We desire that Abraham Lincoln's words shall be fulfilled, that we will highly resolve that the dead shall not have died in vain!

When the new Germany thinks and speaks in this manner it is not in an attitude or spirit of presumption, but it is the expression of a special decree of fate which has struck no other nation so hard, so deeply, so overwhelmingly as

Germany. No other nation shares the same geographical fate as Germany—planted in the very heart of Europe without any natural and secure frontiers. Only on German soil could the scenes be laid of a thirty years' war in which all nations of Europe were involved. No other nation has been so cast down from the dazzling heights of enthroned and envied glory into the dark depths of Daniel's pit. This new Germany understands and interprets the meaning of Daniel's words, 'Weighed, weighed and found wanting', as imposing on her a duty to herself, as well as to Europe and the world.[1] We perceive the obligation to pursue the stony way, to engage in exemplary experience, in educational experiment, to be a kind of laboratory of new ideas. We are determined to pursue this road with eyes open, with true vision, and with confident courage: 'A new day beckons us to new shores!'

What shall be the roads? What shall be the goals? Who shall be the guides?

The German people to-day are convinced that a policy of ideas is more beneficial and of stronger endurance than a policy of might. Napoleon at Elba, looking back at his life and former policy, arrived at the same conclusion, and said: 'Ideas have conquered me'; Emerson expressed the same conviction when he said: 'They only who build on ideas, build for eternity.'

[1] A few weeks after these lectures a new book by Count Keyserling was published by the Reichs-Verlag in Darmstadt: *Die neuentstehende Welt*. I am glad to find in this book the philosophic justification of my political conviction and experience. Count Keyserling demonstrates that we are standing at the gates of a European feeling of community of interests and purposes of a universal age, of an oecumenical culture, and explains that universalism and nationalism at one and the same time represent the polar tension in the new rhythm. Europe to-day is playing the same historic part as Palestine played in the Roman world-empire; here all the vital problems of mankind are crowded together; here and here only the new spirit can develop into and make itself felt as an historical force.

## LECTURE III

What idea? The idea of Right. What is Right? Formerly it was said: Might is Right, or Might goes before Right, or Need abolishes Right. At one time this was also the code of relationship and intercourse between individuals, until community of interests established a Right, a Law applicable to all. The violation of this law excludes the individual from the privileges inherent in that Right, that Law, making him an outlaw. Development of Right in the relation and intercourse between the nations will have to pursue a similar course. Colonel House says in a letter to President Wilson: 'Nations in the future must be governed by the same high code of honour that we demand of individuals.' And Gladstone expressed the hope and the necessity: 'The greatest triumph of our time, a triumph in a region loftier than that of electricity or steam, will be the enthronement of this idea of Public Right as the governing idea of European policy; as the common and precious inheritance of all lands, but superior to the passing opinion of any.'

It is in the nature of things and of human beings that the weaker is the first to appeal to Right against Might, against superior power, against abuse of power. Germany is powerless, disarmed, defenceless, and possesses only one weapon: Right, the right of treaties and of obligations, the right as an idea and as an ideal, the right as might. Out of realism, out of egoism, as well as out of idealism and humanism, this Germany emerges into the policy of right. In France, Briand expressed a similar realism by saying: 'France needs Locarno, because it will be impossible for France to try the feat of 1914 a second time.' In France, also, idealistic forces are mixed with realistic calculation, conjuncture with conviction. Both unite in the one stream: Right, the Policy of Right, the Might of Right.

In this, Germany has recourse to the ideals of the best

period of her existence as a nation. She can appeal to her own organic development, she need not borrow from a different organism.

When Mr. H. G. Wells was in Germany some years ago, he summarized his impressions by saying: 'The German people had been united by the imperialistic idea; this idea was destroyed by the result of the war; now the German people are wandering about like a flock of sheep upon the hill-side, searching for a new goal. The German people must find a connexion with former history, and a new constructive idea from their own development.'

This historical connexion and these constructive ideas have been found. The connexion is that of the old Germanic constitution, which was democratic, and of old imperial times, when for centuries German Emperors were elected by the people, as well as the time of the countless proud and powerful Free Cities, which had republican constitutions of their own. (I repeat, the Hohenzollern Empire lasted only for forty-eight years, less than two generations.) These ideas are the ideals of the time before and after 1848, when German emigration to America was so strong because of democratic convictions, of the time when Germans like Carl Schurz fled to America and became outstanding leaders in that democracy. The new Germany is finding the spiritual connexion with that old Germany, with the ideals of that great Parliament of 1848 in St. Paul's Church in Frankfort, which united the liberal *intelligentsia* of Germany under the black, red, and gold banner of 'Unity and Right and Liberty'.

St. Paul's Church is a living force and is becoming more so every day. Since the time when we, together with Ebert, the President of the Reich, went in solemn procession to St. Paul's Church in March, 1923, on the occasion of the seventy-fifth anniversary of the Parliament of

Frankfort, and since a periodical publication entitled 'St. Paul's Church' has been working to show the German people the connexion between 'Weimar' and 'Frankfort', ever since then it is becoming more and more clear to the German people that 1848 was not a 'Year of Madness', as we were taught at school at one time, nor was it a 'Parliament of Professors and Ideologists' as it was derisively called at a time when the 'Idea' meant nothing, and 'Might' appeared to be everything. The German people have found out that there those German minds were united who prophetically and politically saw the new Germany ahead, and wanted, not only the State of the German people, the greater Germany, in 'Unity and Right and Liberty', but also the disarmed peace of Europe, a Conference of the Nations and even a League of Nations. There is good historic sense in the fact that the first President of the German Republic, Ebert, will now have a monument to his memory close to St. Paul's Church in Frankfort.

Listen to what Carl Vogt (1848) declared there: 'I believe that the ultimate goal of our policy and the greatest problem which we can solve will be the establishment of a disarmed peace in Europe, and I would welcome with joy a newly arisen Germany, able to step forth from the tomb with the palm of peace, and pressing this palm into the hands of every nation on the Continent, of every nation in Europe. ... I believe ... that the time has arrived for the two great nations which constitute the heart of Europe, the French and the Germans, to prepare the way for an alliance such as is meet and right, and united to march onward to meet freedom.'

Or to what Arnold Ruge (1848) said: 'I beg to move, that inasmuch as armed peace by its standing armies has imposed an intolerable burden upon the nations of Europe, and is endangering the liberty of the citizen, we recognize the necessity for convening a conference of the nations, having for its object the general disarmament of Europe. ... The congressional system will only become real and true when those constituting the congresses are elected members of the same by the people: only congresses of the nations are true congresses; congresses of diplomats are false congresses. ... I propose that the thinking German nation should take the initiative in the great idea of general disarmament, and in enjoining this idea on the other nations. ... In every phase of our entire development, even during the period recently passed through, we have shown that we are adverse to militarism; all our revolts were revolts against the military, much more than against the power of the Government and of the monarchy. They were revolts against the military and against the "Junkers", the landed aristocrats in the Army. They indicate the German spirit ... that we demand Liberty of the Subject, and not militarism. ... That the Army should be kept under the careful control of the civil power, and should be governed by the civil power absolutely is the fundamental principle of the American constitution which, introduced by Washington, has been adopted in all constitutions of the federated States, and is a maxim which most certainly must be included in the German constitution, among the maxims governing the attitude of the public, and must certainly also become a maxim of European international law. For we must abolish armed peace, the maintenance of which is an impossibility not only because an armed peace is essentially an impossibility, but because it is a relic of barbarism, an absolutely mistaken method against all order of freedom, against the new order of things, against the democratic and republican order which we wish to establish....'

And lastly, listen to what Hermann von Beckerath (1848)

had to say: ' I agree with the view that these principles will permeate the life of the nations more and more, that they will purify and ennoble the conscience of nationalities, and that ultimately they will lead up to a higher state of human perfection—I should like to call it a general League of Nations.'

The Germans of '48 had precisely the same ideas as a Welshman of '48, namely Henry Richard. It was most impressive for us Germans when we were in London and Aberystwyth this summer (1926) for the conference of the World Federation of the Unions for a League of Nations, and heard of this connexion on an excursion to Tregaron. The only difference is that the Germans of '48 obtained no political influence, whereas the Welshman did. Henry Richard was also active in Germany (after the first peace congress at Brussels in 1848 and after the Paris Congress of 1849), preparing the way for the Frankfort Congress of 1850. He was the founder of international peace congresses and the parliamentary advocate of international arbitration. He faced the plenipotentiaries of the Great Powers in Paris after the Crimean War in 1856, and in Berlin after the Russo-Turkish War in 1878. He was a good Welshman, always 'the member for Wales', as Gladstone called him, and a good European.

At a later date in Germany Nietzsche—after Goethe the best European of the German nation—picked up the same thread of ideas. Nietzsche, who out of Germany is so often incorrectly quoted and misunderstood as the panegyrist of war, is in reality the panegyrist of the battle of the minds and a political pacifist. He actually demands 'that a nation distinguished in war and victory, in supreme perfection of military order and intelligence, and accustomed to make the greatest sacrifices for all these, should voluntarily exclaim: "Let us break our swords asunder!" and that it should utterly destroy its military organization down to the very last foundation-stone.'

And even before 1848 we have Fichte, whose idea of community also extends to a demand for a League of Nations, and before Fichte, Kant, who from the absolutism of the law of right deduces the idea of a general and everlasting peace, a League of Nations, that will come 'even for a nation of devils, if only they have understanding'. Hölderlin and Goethe mean more to the new Germany than to the former generation—not only as poets, but as thinkers and teachers. Something of this spirit finds expression in our new constitution, the only one which expressly demands 'Reconciliation of the nations to be taught in the schools'. The Prussian reorganization of the higher schools now expressly makes 'Europeanism' the main idea of education: the common root and mutual interdependence of European cultures.[1]

[1] Compare : *The Reorganization of the Prussian High Schools*, Berlin 1924, pp. 24 ff. 'If it is desired to use the great epochs of culture, exercising their influence upon German culture, as sources of education for the German nation, then side by side with Christianity and the preceding ancient order of things we must place, at least as equally powerful in its influence, modern Europeanism as it has developed in the course of the history of the modern spirit since the Reformation and the Renaissance, according to the well-defined system of thought, in which to this day all fundamental principles which govern our modern culture have been formed. It is only by a study of this history that the peculiar nature of the German spirit can be properly understood. Its rise was struggle and agreement, chiefly with France and England, both, however, conceived as the indissoluble entity they represent intellectually. . . . For that reason we need an educated class which, capable of dealing conscientiously with these developments and problems, is also capable of leading us in this "Kulturkampf", this struggle of intellects, which ultimately must after all lead us once more to a European synthesis of culture (unless we are content to believe that the West is doomed to destruction), in which we shall press forward anew, giving and receiving, to a new Germanism. The struggle between the nations is at the same time also a predestined union and communion in culture, and the struggle between two different cultures always exercises

## LECTURE III

Another State (Brunswick) goes even farther and exhorts the teachers of history to relegate wars to the background and to explain to the youth that co-operation rather than the struggle for life is the law of animal and human societies, and that every nation is a member of the human family.

But the idea of right, and right itself, only becomes and only is might, when it is organized. The organization of right is one of the goals which new Germany has set herself. Wilson proposed a League of Nations in 1916, for the organization of right. Germany was the first Government which accepted and agreed to such a League. Bethmann Hollweg in 1916 replied, approving the proposals, and Erzberger, in 1917, wrote the first book on and in favour of a League of Nations. In 1918[1] I founded the 'German League of Nations Union' (historically the first organization

also a certain subtle influence and calls for reciprocal action. That this educational thought has not as yet been embodied in a special type of school, notwithstanding its importance, is due to the fact that the economic, technical, and positivist period now behind us was confronted by other tasks and problems. That is also why the study of foreign languages as imparted in our schools failed to reveal the soul of the culture of other nations to the educated youth of the nation. . . . It is obvious that, having this object in view, the teaching of modern languages in our colleges will be determined, ruled, and governed thereby, much in the same way as the colleges specializing in the dead languages were ruled by those languages of antiquity. The development of the unified system of thought governing the nations of modern Europe has transformed to the very core every form of present-day life. One of the most widely extended ruling forces of this modern European spirit is the habit of mathematical, natural scientific reasoning, which was one of the determining factors in forming German idealism not only in Kant but in Goethe also. For this reason it was necessary to amplify and extend this mathematical natural-scientific reasoning considerably in the "Realgymnasium" colleges.'

[1] It is strange and significant that the very same date, September 10, on which I proposed and started the foundation of a German Union for a League of Nations, has become the historical date of the unanimous admission of Germany to the League of Nations in 1926.

of its kind in the world). I founded it because we knew that—no matter what the result of the war, and whoever the so-called victor might be—the time after the world war must belong to a League of Nations, a new organization of international relations and methods. The German Foreign Office drafted a scheme for a League of Nations with the help of persons whose names are known to you: Dr. Simons, at that time legal adviser of the Foreign Office, afterwards Minister for Foreign Affairs, then, between the administration of Ebert and Hindenburg, Acting President, and now President of the Supreme Court (also President of the Board of Trustees of our 'Hochschule für Politik'); Dr. Gaus, now legal adviser of the Foreign Office, and, as you know, a pioneer of Locarno; Dr. Schücking, the well-known expert in international law.

There are many interesting features in this German draft, among others that the Congress of States therein suggested is constituted on the lines of the United States Senate, that is to say, that every State is represented on an equal basis, and that the suggested world parliament is constituted on the same lines as the American House of Representatives, that is to say, each State has its number of representatives in proportion to its population. An oligarchical council was not suggested in the German draft. The German draft demanded open diplomacy, independent arbitration tribunals, a non-political system of mediation and conciliation (carried out actually by the German-Swiss arbitration treaty 1921), instead of the political mediation set up by the Covenant of the League (Art. 12, 14 ff.).

German readiness to agree to the organization of a League of Nations was an actual fact at that time (from 1917 onwards)—based among other reasons on the recognition that it was a piece of German philosophy which was now to become a political reality. Germany remembered that

## LECTURE III

the German philosopher Immanuel Kant[1] as early as 1786 created a League of Nations system, albeit a system of philosophy, a human ideal; a system that has now become a fact, a practical institution, thanks to the statesmanship of Wilson. German preparedness to accept a League of Nations was a fact at that time: after Bethmann-Hollweg, Chancellor Prince Max and, at Versailles, Count Brockdorff-Rantzau made application to enter the League. Then, between 1919 and 1924, there are five years of German scepticism in regard to Geneva, dating back to the rejection of Germany's application, to the combination of the dictated peace of Versailles and the covenant of the League of Nations, and finally to various decisions of the League of Nations against Germany. Germany's first faith in the League of Nations thus ended in disappointment, in mistrust, in rejection by public opinion. Nevertheless, our own circle of the German League of Nations Union, first and last and all the time, made it its duty to educate the German people, and to encourage the German Government in a League of Nations policy. We were and are convinced that Versailles means an end, and Geneva a beginning. Versailles meant war-psychosis, and Geneva means peace-spirit. You will find this difference even in the Covenant of Geneva: Art. 19 places the revision of Versailles under the League of Nations. This is the victory of President Wilson over Clemenceau.

Now let us go from Geneva to another bi-national lake of Switzerland, to Locarno. Even before Germany could become a member of the League of Nations she endeavoured

[1] Cp. Veit Valentin: *Die Geschichte des Völkerbundgedankens in Deutschland* (Verlag Engelmann, Berlin): Leibniz, Christian Wolf, Herder, Lessing, Wieland, Kant, Schelling, Fichte, Fries, Krause, J. J. Wagner, Fr. Schlegel, Novalis, Hegel, Ruge, Schleiermacher, Goerres, Gentz, Jean Paul, L. Boerne, Rotteck, Paul Pfizer, Friedrich List, Schaeffle, Konstantin Frantz, Planck, &c. All of them proposed a League of Nations.

to exemplify and demonstrate this new conception of international relations, this new phase of the idea of right conceived in the sphere of fundamental and theoretical conviction, by practical and political application. It was in this sense that Briand spoke of the moral membership of Germany in the League of Nations. I mean the Security Treaties, the 'Locarno system'.

We are not interested here in individual provisions, articles, and paragraphs; all we are here concerned with is the system of Locarno, the 'spirit of Locarno': the expression of a new mind, the intellectual and political initiative, and finally its historical significance, viewed from the standpoint of the past and intended for the future.

The first fact to be dealt with is that the struggle for the Rhine is a political problem nearly two thousand years old in importance and effect—from the days of the Roman Empire and of the formation of the Germanic State onwards—and about two centuries old in importance and effect in the relations between Germany and France. This struggle is the central problem of central Europe. This struggle had over and over again, for millenniums and centuries, broken out in the form of war and had never been settled.

The second fact: for this, the oldest problem of the Europe of history, a new solution has been sought and has now been found, no longer in the antiquated form of alliances, which provide a false security and spread a certain mistrust which is dangerous; no longer in the antiquated form of a 'balance' of power, which alternately menaces others or feels itself menaced by others; but in a new system, mutually desired and created by all parties concerned, based upon mutual understanding and confidence, which lays down a rule prohibiting war, for the first time in the world's history, and substitutes mutual international protection for national self-defence.

That is Locarno, the system and the spirit of Locarno. It is based upon the idea, not that the two sides expect to fight, but that they believe in one another's good faith and good will and expect to agree. Locarno means a symbol of the new age; of the attempt at a synthesis of nationality and supernationality, of nationalism and universalism. That is what Stresemann meant in saying: 'Locarno is not only a legal construction of a political idea, but the basis of a new system of the European idea.' And Briand: 'In consequence of these treaties we become and are European. The sectionalism of our countries is from henceforth abolished and extinguished.' Sir Austen Chamberlain, the third of the Locarno trinity, the godfather of the Franco-German agreement, expressed himself in a similar way.

The third fact: the initiative for such a conception of a new mind and spirit, for such a new form and order of regulations between nations, emanated from Germany, although by this initiative Germany acknowledged a *status quo* involving national losses in the west and in the east, the loss of national territories of the old Germany. But 'material losses must be made good on the spiritual plane'.

Compare 1871 and 1925: after the Franco-German War and the Treaty of Frankfort Gambetta preaching revenge in order to regain Alsace-Lorraine, and now, after the world war and through Locarno, Hindenburg signing renunciation of Alsace-Lorraine in order to co-operate with France.

This single fact attests more than any commentary the European spirit of this new Germany. As further evidence there are the arbitration treaties which Germany has concluded with almost all her neighbours. Germany is resolved to promote the World Court at the Hague, set up by

Art. 14 of the Covenant, and to promote non-political mediation.[1]

[1] This German mission was foreseen and forecast with prophetic insight by the poet Gerhart Hauptmann in his Festival Play on the occasion of the centenary of 1813. It is true that at that time Imperial Germany rejected this Festival Play. Republican Germany made it the Festival Play of the first anniversary of Constitution Day in 1920, in the presence of President Ebert in the former Royal Theatre, now State Theatre. This prophetic play thus describes Europe :

'Not yet are you delivered.—You still bear the burden of the unborn Son of God.

Europe's Prince of Peace is not yet born. The Saviour is not yet—though many temples have been dedicated to him. . . .

And yet, I see the distant dawn of the Day of Peace.—I see it—notwithstanding the intensity of the poisonous pestilence, of the sinister madness raging in the blood of Europe.'

Hauptmann describes the future of Germany, which, as Athene-Germany, speaks thus : 'Nevertheless, I feel with my whole Being, that I understand the meaning of the weapons of my Inner Being—of my mind and soul. These weapons are deeds of Peace and nevermore the deeds of War.

I desire Good and not Evil.

What is War but stark murder ?

I call upon you to create a new warrior—a warrior who brings Life—not Death.

Then will man be united with man, and peoples with peoples. Across chasms will they be united.—Loaded caravans will travel, laden with costly wares, instead of with the burden of dissensions.

There, where I am and whither you strive—there is the light.

Never separated, but for ever united, we know nothing of War.—Thus does peace dwell among us ; not here nor there—not limited by us, like an angel host, protecting its ruler.—

No, our souls are one with his soul.

We are not divided by language nor by stream nor by ocean.

Those who have at heart the salvation of mankind cannot be parted by the gods or by the Unknown God.

What separates mankind is Error—Error which alone lets loose Hatred and Ignorance and stark starvation.

Mankind is not divided by the Divine which dwells within it.

For the Divine is Eros.

Eros is the Creator—the Generator.'

[I am indebted to Mrs. Everard Hopkins for this translation. The German original will be found in an Appendix.—E. J.]

## LECTURE III

The necessity and possibility of a 'Security Pact' was a research work of our Hochschule für Politik (School of Politics). Three days after the occupation of the Ruhr by the French, we formed in our Institute a committee to deal with the situation: Dr. Walther Simons (Chief Judge), Dr. Hans Simons (his son and the Director of our Hochschule für Politik), Dr. Preuss (the author of the new Constitution), Dr. Schücking, and Dr. Riedl (the Austrian Minister at Berlin). The conclusion we arrived at was, that neither coal nor iron nor economic demands were the main problem, but a politico-psychological question, namely the French feeling of insecurity (a feeling expressed by the famous sentence of Clemenceau: 'There are twenty millions of Germans too many'), that has no foundation in fact, but is nevertheless a political fact. So we tried to find a preventive medicine and we worked out, in the seclusion of our Institute, not a memorandum, but a formal treaty; a 'Treaty of Security' we called it among ourselves. We submitted it to our Foreign Office. This draft went much farther than the Treaty of Locarno: while that treaty solved only political problems, our draft worked out also the economic co-operation of the powers concerned (customs, trade, transport).

A characteristic feature of European development in general, as for France and England on the one hand and Germany on the other, is shown by a brief analysis of the course taken by the idea of security.

In 1918 and 1919 a French memorial by Clemenceau and Foch was addressed to Wilson on the separation from Germany of the left bank of the Rhine, but rejected by Wilson and Lloyd George.

1919. Treaty of Versailles.

1919. French attempt at an Anglo-French-American Alliance against Germany.

1922 and 1923. French attempt at an Anglo-French Alliance against Germany.

1923. German initiative (during the occupation of the Ruhr, 2nd May) and attempt at a Rhine pact, providing for arbitration or settlement by mutual agreement on the lines of the Bryan treaties, abruptly rejected by Poincaré (6th of May).

1925. 9th of February. New presentation of the German memorandum at Paris and London.

20th of February. Acceptance of the principle by France.

5th of October. Beginning of Locarno.

16th of October. Conclusion of Locarno with the historical statement, 'War is crime!'

'Here and to-day begins a new epoch of world history— and you can boast that you were present at its birth', said Goethe after the battle of Valmy during the French Revolution. Locarno is more than Valmy. Locarno is a revolutionary system of international relationship, a deliberate process, constructive and creative.

In order to understand the realistic sound basis of the German philosophy of Locarno you must consider three facts about Germany and three facts concerning Europe:

(1) No other nation is as devoid of natural boundaries as Germany: open in all directions, never and nowhere protected, and now even disarmed.

(2) No other nation has as many neighbours as Germany, namely 16: each single one of the larger ones superior to Germany by armaments and alliances.

(3) No other nation has her co-nationals as dispersed as Germany: among 16 neighbouring and adjoining States.

Connect these facts about Germany with three facts concerning Europe, and you will have Germany's fate and decision:

(1) The Treaty of Versailles has divided Europe into

more so-called national States than ever existed before (30 instead of 18).

(2) Not one of these new States was built on economic efficiency, but on political prejudices.

(3) Not one of these new States is a homogeneous State of one nation; each one is composed of various nationalities (minorities).

What do these hard facts and realities mean? For Europe a mutual interdependence, and for Germany that she is the interdependent centre of the European interdependence, the most insecure nation, the most internationally located nation. Germany is the centre of all European problems concerned—not by choice, not by fortune, but by geographical fate and even more since Versailles than ever before. This geographical fate is the decisive political fact for Germany and for Europe.

The Locarno system is already foreshadowed in another treaty with an Italian name, in the Treaty of Rapallo between Germany and Russia, in 1922, which ultimately led to the Berlin Treaty of 1926. The only thing that Rapallo can be reproached with is that it was concluded in the neighbourhood of Genoa, and at the same time as the Conference of Genoa: not its contents, nor its tendency, but only its time and place. Rapallo was the first conference since Versailles which began to assume the aspect of a peace conference. But mistrust still supervened. This mistrust led to Rapallo being misunderstood: as though the treaty were an alliance and a treaty of aggression between Germany and Russia against Poland and France. In reality, Rapallo was the first peace treaty: the first because it knew nothing about either victor or vanquished; because it was not a dictated treaty, but the outcome of negotiations and understanding on an equal basis; because it drew a red line under the account of the war, by mutual abandonment of war debts; and because it really established peace by mutual resumption of diplomatic relations and representatives in Berlin and in Moscow, in mutual goodwill, regulating economic relations by most-favoured-nation treatment. That was all. But the Conference of Genoa collapsed because of mistrust, and we packed up our trunks.

Not exactly the same kind of mistrust, but something similar, has now arisen on account of the expansion of the Rapallo Treaty into the Treaty of Berlin: once again, as though the latter were an alliance, and a war treaty. Precisely the opposite is the truth. Briand, too, assured the French Senate that Germany could not be reproached for having signed the treaty, saying: 'It is an absolutely pacific treaty, and it interferes in no wise with the obligations of Locarno.' The Berlin Treaty not only does not interfere with Locarno, but on the contrary expands, amplifies Locarno. Germany is the centre of Europe between West and East, a kind of bridge. Germany expands Locarno from the West to the East. The Treaty of Berlin appears as a synthesis of Geneva and the Hague, of the policy of the League and of international law. Germany engages not to take part in any hostile actions against a peaceful Russia; in which connexion Germany, alone, has the right to decide whether Russia's intentions are peaceful or warlike. And, inversely, Russia undertakes the same obligations as regards Germany. Both States secure to each other the conclusion of an Arbitration Treaty. On this, Mr. J. L. Garvin wrote: 'If the League of Nations succeeds, there will be no great war, and meanwhile the agreement between Germany and the Soviet Republic not to nourish hostilities against either is no menace to peace, but its reinforcement.' Mr. Garvin adds, that 'an offensive and defensive alliance, directed by the Kremlin chiefly against the British Empire, was bound to be rejected without a moment's hesitation by so gracious a government as that to which Herr Stresemann belongs. The milder pact into which Germany has actually entered is legitimate from every point of view.'

A comparison with the old Berlin Treaty of 1878 characterizes the progress of the new Berlin Treaty. 1878 led to the German-Austrian Alliance, to the Triple Alliance, to the division of Europe into two sections, to that system of alliances, armaments, and attempts at establishing 'balance of power' which led to the world war. There is another essential difference between the Berlin of 1878 and the Berlin of 1926: the former treaties were a deep and hidden secret, and this treaty is a world-wide open fact.

What do these facts express? A new Germany and a new Europe; the problem of a new order of the community of nations and an attempt at a solution of the problem; a new system of international relations by new methods and by a new machinery.

What was the technical procedure in previous conflicts? Ultimatum, mobilization, beginning of war. The precision and adjustment of that machine was such, that it had to reckon with minutes. One minute after the expiration of the hour fixed in the ultimatum, hostilities started, and the whole mechanism of alliance and armament policy ran its course automatically with the precision of an elaborate clockwork.

To lose no time—that was the watchword of that old negative method, so that the enemy may gain no advantage; in other words, to enkindle the passions and to fan the flames thereof.

To gain time—that is the watchword of this new positive method, to allow the tempers of the disputants to cool, to quiet and calm the passions. Consequently: round table, proposals, agreement, arbitration.

Whereas formerly decisions made in a few minutes rendered war possible and necessary, now decisions which will take months to arrive at will render war impossible and unnecessary. Even Serajevo would not have let loose the dogs of world war, if at that time, twelve years ago, this new method conceived and born in post-war times, had been in existence. But the mental habit of that time stuck to the sovereignty of the powers which were eager not to give up their sovereignty, it stuck to the discrimination between great powers and small nations, so that a great power declined to meet at the same round table a small nation. The terrible success of prestige was at stake.

Like Locarno, Geneva is both a system and a spirit, a machinery to settle the result of conflicts, and an atmosphere to avoid their causes. All through history, up to the world war, the statesmen of different countries had never come together regularly or learnt to know one another's minds. Poincaré and Grey, for instance, never met Bethmann-Hollweg. Ambassadors used to meet after catastrophes in order to settle their consequences, but statesmen never met before a crisis in order to deal with its causes. Now they are becoming accustomed to meeting not occasionally but regularly to talk questions over before they become troublesome, to enter into personal contact, to develop mutual understanding and co-operation, as members of an International Parliament or Council. This method would have averted the world war.

Humanity needs the experience of the world war in order to understand that it is necessary to avoid a repetition of its futility. Men needed the experience of a world war in order to grasp the fact that after a war there are no such things as victors but only vanquished. In talking to

Mr. Norman Angell about his *Great Illusion* and the truth of his prophecy, he reminded me that he had distinctly stated in his book that this prophecy would nevertheless not prevent war, as humanity at large and man as an individual only learn by experience, by their own sufferings. Or in a word of Prudhommeaux: 'We shall never abolish war till we have realized what it means.'

To-day the German mark is stabilized, and is the only stable currency of the European continent, while the French franc is not yet stabilized. Germany, who lost the war, has won her new mark; France, who won the war, is losing her old franc. And furthermore, Germany is not by any means gloating over the predicament of France. Germany knows that her interests are closely bound up with those of France. German industry, trade, and export suffer on account of French inflation. Germany's obligations in the matter of Reparations give her an interest in French economic conditions. Germany knows that her currency could only be established by an international community of interests, by inter-governmental assistance, by the Dawes plan, which I call a life insurance for Germany. That is its political significance; while its economic wisdom will be characterized by its flexibility providing for final readjustment in a new European atmosphere. This, Vice-President Dawes in his own characteristic way summarized in the course of an interview with me in Washington, as follows: 'The only definite thing about the Dawes plan is the fact that it is not definite.'

One of these days France too will know that French currency is a matter of international community of interests, for inter-governmental assistance. The European powers will realize that ' they hang together or hang separately '.

In short, whichever way we turn, in every direction we see the same outlook of companionship in misfortune and fortune, the interdependence of interests of nations, and, conversely, the constraint upon the predominance of any one nation by a commonwealth of many, whether it be the League of Nations, arbitration courts, or the linking together of individual nations. The fact of the matter is, this great world of ours has become very small. The times of Columbus, who took several months to get to America, are not the times of a Zeppelin airship, which only takes a few days. The times in which the transatlantic cable is becoming a trans-continental telephone have transformed the universe into one single homogeneous continent. New world-wide wireless has lessened old world-wide distances of oceans and continents.

All that does not mean 'internationalism'. There is no need for any nation to sacrifice its character, its nature, its note, its peculiar gifts, qualities, varieties. On the contrary, it is its duty to develop them, to improve them, in order to be able to contribute all the more richly towards the unity, community, and the vitality of all, to a polyphony and symphony.

This new Germany of ours is now more than ever justified in proclaiming the sentiments expressed in her National Anthem: 'Deutschland, Deutschland über Alles', that national song of the democrats of 1848 which lays down the most beautiful principle of all: Unity and Right and Liberty. It was not mere chance, but imbued with a significant historical meaning, that the first President of our democratic republic—Ebert—proclaimed this expression of an 1848 democrat, Hoffmann von Fallersleben, as the National Anthem, whereas before, during the monarchy, it was an occasional anthem, after and in addition to the Kaiser Anthem. By the way those words, 'Deutschland, Deutschland über Alles' have frequently been misunderstood abroad and are still misunderstood.

To us Germans, literally and spiritually, they simply mean 'God save Germany' and 'God will save Germany provided she is a Germany of unity and right and liberty'.

As I said, there is no call upon any nation to sacrifice itself. Supernationalism—universalism of that particular type—means renunciation of egoism and chauvinism and acknowledgement of the higher significance of communion, of co-operation. It means acknowledgement of the fact that the historical mission of our age will be to develop the antithesis of nationalism and universalism into a synthesis, a new rhythm. The new universalism is the consequence of general mutual interdependence of all, economically, politically, nationally. This new universalism acknowledges the individuality of the nation, but at the same time understands the community of a family of nations.

That phrase of Briand, which I quoted, is also a saying of Goethe: 'To be a good German means being a good European.' Another German, Adam Müller, stated in 1806 after the German defeat: 'Not in the suppression, but in the greatest prosperity and development of our neighbours shall we find our own happiness. We will not live by exalting ourselves nor by boasting of our strength compared with the strength of other nations. We do not desire to progress by reason of their falling behind in the struggle, but as constant mediators to secure our own and their common progress.' Nietzsche, too, said: 'Europe wishes to become one. Every man of any depth and breadth of mind, who has lived during our century, has yearned for this great spiritual achievement, has sought to open a way to this new synthesis, has striven to realize in himself the European of the future.'

To-day this new synthesis is not only a matter for the individual, and not merely a desire of the philosopher, but is also the goal of political leaders and a task to be performed by the nations. Similar ideas have always existed among all peoples, among all leaders throughout all time, but always at different times: once here or there, but never here and there and everywhere. That is the point to-day: the time is ripe, and the world also is ripe. The spirit of our age is at the same time the spirit of our world. The revelations to the prophets of old have become the commonplaces of the newspapers.

That does not necessarily mean ' Pan-Europe ', nor ' United States of Europe ', not even a European Customs Union [1] for to-morrow or the next day, not a wide-reaching economic entente, but it does, at least, mean a removal of many artificial barriers that now impede economic intercourse between two or more group unions. It means the recognition of the necessity for common action in economic and financial problems, problems of production and consumption, transport problems, and so on, in which there is interdependence of interests and of States, a real and true interdependence instead of a supposed and false self-sufficiency, first of all, between Germany and France, then between other nations. The Franco-German relationship is the point of intersection of the European diagonals, the fulcrum of the European system. Franco-German antagonism had divided Europe into two groups; Franco-German co-operation will create a new European co-operation. But economic co-operation will be possible only after a political agreement. Economic interests can and will prepare a political agreement, but political confidence is needed before economic partnership.

Let me tell you an experience I had in America in the train. I was preparing my lecture and was using a dictionary. A passenger recognized me as a German and addressed me. He was an American born in England,

---

[1] Compare *Europäische Zollunion*, twenty-two articles, published by Dr. Hanns Heiman (Berlin, Hobbing).

educated in Germany, and during the war he had fought in France. We talked, and he showed me a small book with a long title: 'How to use human common sense in the best way', written by a French philosopher (Descartes), translated and printed by a German publisher, read and lost by a German soldier on the French battlefield, found and read by this English-American soldier. Let us look upon the fate of this book as our own fate and aim: to use human common sense in the best way. That means not for destruction, but for construction, for co-operation.

In conclusion, just a few words on Germany in the League of Nations. Here we have to distinguish between two problems. First: Germany's work for the League of Nations, that is to say, to help develop it into a democratic and universal body. That the League's present structure is not an ideal one many events have shown, especially the crisis in the spring of 1926. Nor could it very well be otherwise, because a League of Nations conceived and born in the period of war-psychology must bear the marks of a war child. The discrimination between victors and vanquished, great powers and small nations, must vanish. The principle of democracy must overcome the practice of oligarchy, not through moral menace, nor bargain, but through performance and conviction.

And the second task to be performed by Germany is to represent and stand up for her political ideas in the League of Nations, in short, to strive for the Fourteen Points of President Wilson. In this connexion I distinguish three main points:

(1) Disarmament or limitation of armaments. We know that this is an extremely difficult problem, but here, too, Germany is an educational experiment. We not only have the right, but it is our bounden duty, to champion the cause of disarmament and to co-operate to the end, that, in keeping

with the Treaty of Versailles and the Covenant of the League of Nations, other States, too, should restrict their armaments. We understand the connexion between disarmament and security and know that the one is impossible without the other.

(2) The minorities problem. Germany is the only great nation which is not yet a national whole, to-day even less than before the war. About twelve million Germans, all along the frontiers of Germany, are citizens of non-German States.[1] Germany is the country of the centre as well as the land of 'irredenta' par excellence. The new Germany renounces every kind of 'irredentist' policy, of 'unredeemed lands'. She does not want any 'release', any separations of these Germans from neighbouring States, or their incorporation in her own, but she champions the cause of cultural autonomy for German communities in other States, that is to say, the right of a section of the population to its own language, schools, and church, to its own intellectual culture. Germany conceives it to be her duty and takes pride in granting to the minorities in Germany such a measure of cultural autonomy as she herself claims in like manner for German minorities in the neighbouring States. The new constitution expressly demands: 'Non-German-speaking sections of the people are not to be interfered with, either by legislation or administration, in their free national development, least of all in the use of their native tongue in education, in home affairs, and in the administration of justice.' True and fruitful nationalism is that which possesses a feeling not

[1] The 80 million Germans who live in Central Europe are divided among 17 States: 65 millions in Germany, 3 millions in Switzerland, the remaining 12 millions in neighbouring States: Austria, Czecho-Slovakia, Italy, Danzig, Poland, Esthonia, Latvia, Lithuania, Denmark, Belgium, Luxemburg, and France, and in the adjoining parts of former Austria: Hungary, Yugoslavia, and Roumania.

only for its own nationality, but also for the nationality of others, and for that which develops the national State into a State of and for the people, into a true commonwealth. A national policy such as that is the only one capable of insuring international peace.

(3) The union of Germany with German-speaking Austria. We are convinced that the Treaty of Versailles and the principles of democratic self-determination do not preclude the possibility of the union of these two sections of a once-united German people, which were only separated from each other by the personal interests of the two dynasties, the Hohenzollerns and the Habsburgs. The dynasties have disappeared, the peoples have remained. That the road leading to this development and consummation leads by way of the League of Nations only, all of us know. The new Security System of Locarno dispels all previous misgivings of the significance of this union. Such a united State of the German people would consummate the German ideal of the men of 1848: 'Unity and Right and Liberty.'

The new Germany vows allegiance to the ideas of the men of 1848 and to President Wilson's Fourteen Points. He who takes the trouble to compare the 'Forty-Eighters' and the Fourteen Points will find that they do not contradict each other at all, but that they confirm and supplement each other.

The Germany of to-day has entered upon its new path against its will and reluctantly, forced to make a virtue of necessity. But Germany has now found its bearings, and is going ahead along the lines I have tried to draw. We belong to that generation 'which strives from obscurity to light'. We remember a word of the German historian Treitschke: 'Happy the generation upon which cruel necessity imposes a high political idea, great and simple, universally intelligible, drawing all other ideas into its orbit.'

This new Germany is breathing, living, growing up every day.

I spoke about economic experience and political consequences. That is for many, perhaps for most people, the road to be pursued, gradual development into a new attitude of mind, the turning back from the old ways. But it is not the only road, not even the safe road. Nevertheless, it is one road to the goal before us. Here as elsewhere the old saying still applies: All roads lead to Rome, to the Rome of international faith and goodwill.

Developments seem to me to have run on the following lines. The long war came to an end and the so-called peace, which really was the continuation of the war, began with purely military methods of reasoning: military security, military occupation, military oppression.

Slowly, very slowly, economic calculation and consideration followed as a consequence of economic devastation, here, there, and everywhere, in production and consumption, in industry and trade of every nation concerned, not simultaneously, but one after the other with inexorable regularity. And, in the end, economic separation is overthrown in favour of economic co-operation. That is the first turning in the road.

In other words, military reasoning experiences its 'Damascus'. The military Saul is converted into Paul. The military authorities disarm, converted by the possibilities presented by modern technical science. The economic authorities arm themselves, converted by the necessities of economic reorganization. But at first, they also act only in a spirit of private egotism and of merely national calculation, of convenience, not of conviction.

The military people are preparing the disarmament of the nations, political economists are preparing economic agreements. Military disarmament is not enough, economic agreements are not enough.

What is needed is intellectual disarmament, intellectual agreement. 'Man lives not by bread alone.' 'It is the spirit that gives life.' Not only the calculation evolved in the brain, but a vision proceeding from the soul. Not the common need of all, the exhaustion of all, the solidarity of poverty, but the joint will to unity, community, and co-operation, to a new spirit. Not the false preventive measure of the Latin proverb: 'Si vis pacem, para bellum', 'To preserve peace, prepare for war', which turned the armed peace to calculated war, but the constructive idea of the Latin warning that when one member suffers the whole body suffers. We learned both Latin quotations at school, but hitherto only understood and practised the first and not the second.

The need is great for such a new spirit within us, not the arrogance of the chosen nation, but humility in the service of mankind. 'Le droit doit être le souverain du monde' (Mirabeau). Not 'right or wrong—my country!'— not the right of judging in one's own case, but the right of justice—by agreement and by arbitration. That spirit has arisen. That seed is swelling and forging upwards in the soil of every nation. Let us all be gardeners, watchful and diligent, with an understanding of the inexorable organic laws of life and growth, industrious and persevering, tenacious and patient. It is not the impatient will of man that leads from seed to mature plant, but the organic law of life. It is not organization that is the Alpha and Omega of everything, but it is organic force. Only he who knows the organism is capable also of developing it, of organizing the organic forces, as does a skilful gardener. International organization is necessary, but supernational spirit is vital.

As yet the world resembles a solitude, a wilderness, a 'tohuwabohu', empty, without form and void, desolated and destroyed. But already the spirit of creation is moving upon the waters, and a new world is being evolved, a new order out of the anarchy, the chaos, of the seething elements. As yet we are still in the dawn of the first days, but we feel a new atmosphere. He who has ears to hear, hears the beating of the wings of the seventh day: beyond the old chaos the new cosmos. He who has eyes to see, can see beyond the killing and errant Cain and beyond the malevolent confusion of the Tower of Babel a new spirit, the new spirit of Pentecost, of the Pentecost of the man who is a citizen of his nation and a citizen of the community of nations, of the man who no longer reasons egocentrically but cosmocentrically, not only nationally but also supernationally.

Let us, all of us, be filled, inflamed with this spirit of Pentecost, this will: the rising generation, the makers of the future—and, of the older generation those who have learned wisdom from the past and have vision for the future—for the benefit of the present and the future alike, for a better present and a securer future.

# APPENDIX TO LECTURE III

See page 86.

## Gerhart Hauptmann's Prophecy of Germany's Mission for Peace addressed to Europe, 1913

' Noch immer bist Du nicht entbunden, und die Last des ungeborenen Gottessohnes trägst Du noch. Noch nicht geboren ist Europens Friedensfürst, nicht der Erlöser, ob man viele Tempel auch ihm schon geweiht. ... Allein ich sehe dämmern fern des Friedens Tag, so sehr die giftige Pestilenz auch heute noch, und finstrer Wahnsinn, toben in Europens Blut.'

Germany as Athene answering:

' Und alldurchdringend, mich durchdringend allzugleich,
erkenn' ich meines Daseins, meiner Waffen Sinn:
die Tat des Friedens ist es, nicht die Tat des Kriegs.
Die Wohltat ist es! Nimmermehr die Missetat!
Was andres aber ist des Krieges nackter Mord?
So ruf' ich euch denn auf, ihr eines andern
Krieges Krieger! Ihr, nicht todbringend, Leben Schaffende.
... Nun eint sich über Klüfte hin so Mensch zu Mensch,
wie Volk zu Volk. Beladene Karawanen ziehn
köstlich belastet, ausser mit der Zwietracht Last.
... Dort, wo ich bin und wo ihr zuströmt, ist das Licht:
wir nie Getrennten, stets Geeinten, wissen nichts
von Krieg. Und also wohnt der Friede unter uns!
Nicht da, nicht dort und etwa nicht umringt von uns,
wie einer heiligen Schar, die einen Herrscher schützt,
nein! Unsere Seelen sind in seiner Seele eins!
Uns trennen Sprachen, trennen Strom und Meere nicht.
Nicht trennen Götter, noch der unbekannte Gott,
die, denen aller Menschen Heil am Herzen liegt.
Was trennt, ist Irrtum, Irrtum, der allein den Hass
entfesselt, ist Unwissenheit, ist nackte Not
des Hungers! Nicht was Göttliches im Menschen wohnt.
Denn dieses Göttliche ist Eros! Eros ist
der Schaffende! der Schöpfer ...'

PRINTED IN ENGLAND AT THE
UNIVERSITY PRESS, OXFORD
BY JOHN JOHNSON
PRINTER TO THE UNIVERSITY